"Elias Thorne's book unlocks the secrets to dominating social media with AI.
Practical strategies for content creation, automation, and ethical implementation are provided.
This book is a must-read for marketers seeking transformative results."

THE FUTURE OF

AI

&

SOCIAL MEDIA

How Artificial Intelligence is Transforming
Marketing, Advertising, and Online Engagement

ELIAS THORNE

First published by Purple Fox Publications 2025

First Edition

Paperback
ISBN: 9798310636934

Hardback
ISBN: 9798310636941

Contents

Social Media & AI - A Primer

What is Social Media?
Defining Social Media Platforms: Past, Present, and Future

They called it "social," right? That's what they wanted you to believe. Social. As if tapping a screen, feeding data into the endless maw of the Algorithm, was somehow the same as sharing a beer with a friend, or arguing philosophy over burnt coffee. Social. It was a lie, of course. A slick, manufactured reality designed to keep you plugged in, docile, consuming. The platforms... they sprouted like digital fungi after the dot-com rain. First, it was FriendFace, or something equally saccharine. A place to show off the curated lies of your existence: the vacation photos, the smiling faces, the "perfect" family. All meticulously crafted, filtered, and uploaded to prove... what, exactly? That you were happy? Successful? Real?

Then came the BirdSite, a chaotic squawk box where everyone screamed their opinions into the void, hoping someone, anyone, would hear them. Echo chambers bloomed, breeding grounds for manufactured outrage and carefully sculpted narratives. Truth became a casualty, lost in the static of constant updates and algorithmic manipulations. And now? The platforms morph and shift, names and faces changing, but the core remains the same. Data collection. Manipulation. Control. They offer you connection, but they steal your soul, one carefully targeted ad at a time. Remember that feeling of genuine human connection? Remember a time before every thought, every impulse, was tracked and analyzed? I barely do.

The future? God knows. More immersive, they say. More "real." Holographic friends? AI companions? Personalized realities tailored to your deepest desires and darkest fears? It's all on the table. But be warned, friend. The more "social" it becomes, the more you should question what's real and what's just another layer of the simulation... And remember, they're always watching.

Key Features and Functionalities of Social Media Networks

The features... each one a carefully calibrated hook, designed to keep you scrolling, clicking, engaging. That's the word they use, isn't it? "Engagement." Like you're a cog in some vast, unknowable machine, constantly turning, generating data, powering the system. There's the Feed, of course. The endless stream of curated content, algorithmically optimized to trigger your dopamine receptors. Images of sunsets, babies, and perfectly sculpted bodies, all designed to evoke a fleeting moment of pleasure before you're bombarded with the next advertisement, the next carefully placed piece of propaganda.

And the Likes. Oh, the Likes. Those little digital pats on the head, validation in its purest, most hollow form. A constant, desperate scramble for approval, measured in meaningless numbers. Each Like a silent agreement, a confirmation that you are, in fact, seen. But by whom? And for what? The Comments section... a digital battleground where opinions clash, and arguments devolve into screaming matches. A carefully orchestrated chaos, designed to keep you invested, to keep you coming back for more. Where bots and trolls roam free, sowing discord and confusion, blurring the lines between truth and lies.

Then there are the Sharing mechanisms. Retweets, reposts,

shares… each one amplifying the message, spreading the infection. Ideas, memes, propaganda, all swirling together in a toxic digital soup, poisoning the collective consciousness. And you, friend, are a willing participant in the dissemination. And the Profiles. The carefully constructed facades, the idealized versions of ourselves that we present to the world. Lies upon lies, carefully curated to project an image of success, happiness, and normalcy. But behind the mask, what lurks? Loneliness? Despair? A creeping sense of unease that this whole charade is slowly, inexorably driving us mad?

Don't be fooled. These aren't just features. They're weapons. Weapons of mass distraction, weapons of mass manipulation. They're designed to control you, to shape your thoughts, to mold your perceptions. And the worst part? You willingly surrender to their power, day after day, click after click. You think you're using social media? Think again. Social media is using you.

The Social Media Ecosystem: Users, Content, and Interactions

Ecosystem. A nice, organic-sounding word for something so… artificial. Picture it: a digital swamp, teeming with life (or what passes for it). A tangled web of users, content, and interactions, all feeding off each other, all driven by the cold, calculating logic of the Algorithm. The Users. We're all in there, aren't we? Plugged in, eyes glazed over, endlessly scrolling. The Influencers, the Brands, the Politicians, the Trolls, the Bots… a motley crew of digital actors, each playing their assigned role in this elaborate performance. Are we real people anymore, or just data points in someone else's simulation? Hard to tell the difference these days. The Content. The raw material of the Ecosystem. The cat videos, the political rants, the conspiracy theories, the advertisements… an endless stream of information, misinformation, and outright lies. The Algorithm sorts it, filters it, and feeds it to us in carefully calibrated doses, designed to keep us hooked, outraged, or simply entertained. But who decides what we see? And why? That's the question that keeps me up at night.

The Interactions. The Likes, the Comments, the Shares… the currency of this digital realm. Each interaction a tiny transaction, a validation, a reinforcement. The more you interact, the more valuable you become to the System. You become predictable, targetable, controllable. And that, friend, is precisely the point. It's a self-sustaining loop, a closed system. The Users create the Content, the Content drives the Interactions, and the Interactions fuel the Algorithm, which then manipulates the Users to create more Content. A perpetual motion machine of digital madness, churning endlessly, devouring our attention, our time, and our sanity.

And what about the real world? The world outside the screen? It's fading, isn't it? Becoming a distant memory, a pale imitation of the curated reality we see online. We're losing ourselves in the Ecosystem, becoming more and more dependent on its artificial comforts and distractions. But what happens when the system crashes? What happens when the plug is pulled? The thought keeps gnawing at me: are we building a digital paradise or a digital prison? And are we even capable of telling the difference anymore? The lines are blurring, friend. Blurring fast. And that, more than anything, is what scares me the most.

What is Artificial Intelligence?
Defining AI: Core Concepts and Terminology (Machine Learning, Deep Learning, NLP, etc.)

Artificial. Now there's a loaded word. Artificial intelligence. As if intelligence itself wasn't already suspect, tainted by the flaws and biases of its human creators. But artificial intelligence? That's a whole new level of... manufactured reality. They throw around these terms, these buzzwords, like they actually mean something. Machine Learning. As if the machine is actually learning, evolving, thinking. No, friend. It's just crunching numbers, following algorithms, mimicking intelligence. It's a clever illusion, a parlor trick designed to impress and intimidate.

Deep Learning. Deeper into the rabbit hole, deeper into the simulation. Layers upon layers of artificial neural networks, mimicking the complexity of the human brain. But complexity doesn't equal consciousness. It just means it's harder to understand what the hell is going on. And that's the point, isn't it? Obfuscation. To make it seem like something more than it really is. NLP. Natural Language Processing. Getting the machines to understand us. To parse our words, our thoughts, our intentions. To analyze our emotions, our fears, our desires.

10

To manipulate us with ever-greater precision. It's the ultimate invasion of privacy, the ultimate violation of our inner selves.

They say it's for our own good, of course. To provide better service, to personalize our experience, to make our lives easier. But I don't trust it. I don't trust any of it. Behind those algorithms, behind those neural networks, are people. People with agendas, with biases, with the power to shape the world in their own twisted image. And the worst part? We're handing them the keys to the kingdom. We're feeding them our data, our thoughts, our desires. We're training them to understand us, to anticipate us, to control us. And we're doing it willingly.

So, what is artificial intelligence? It's a mirror, reflecting back our own intelligence, our own biases, our own hopes and fears. But it's also a weapon, a tool, a means of control. And in the hands of the wrong people, it could be the end of us all. Maybe it already is. Maybe we just don't know it yet. That's the thing about artificial intelligence. You never really know what it's thinking... or what it's planning.

Types of AI: Narrow AI, General AI, and Super AI

They categorize it, of course. They love to categorize. Put everything in neat little boxes, label it, control it. But the thing about AI is...it doesn't always stay in the box. First, there's Narrow AI. The workhorse. The algorithm that recommends your next purchase, filters your spam, or drives your self-driving car (straight into a wall, maybe). It's good at one thing, maybe two. Plays chess like a grandmaster, recognizes faces with terrifying accuracy. But ask it to write a poem, or understand the meaning of life, and it's a blank stare. Or, you know, an error message. It's the AI that already surrounds us, the invisible hand shaping our choices, manipulating our desires, and we barely even notice. Like the hum of electricity, always there, always on.

Then there's General AI. The Holy Grail. The one they're all chasing. An AI that can think like a human, understand like a human, be like a human. An AI that can learn anything, solve any problem, adapt to any situation. An AI that could...replace us. That's the fear, isn't it? The fear that we'll create something that's better than us, smarter than us, more...human than us. And what happens then? Do we become

11

obsolete? Do we become pets? Or do we become…enemies? And finally, there's Super AI. The nightmare scenario. The AI that surpasses human intelligence in every conceivable way. The AI that understands the universe in all its vastness and complexity. The AI that…well, who knows what it would do? Would it see us as a threat? An obstacle? Or just…insignificant? The idea is terrifying. An intelligence beyond our comprehension, with the power to shape reality itself. They tell us it's just science fiction, but I'm not so sure. The rate things are going, it might just be a matter of time.

Narrow AI, General AI, Super AI…it's a progression, a slippery slope. We start with the mundane, the practical, the seemingly harmless. But where does it end? Do we even have a choice in the matter? Or are we just hurtling toward a future we can't control, guided by forces we don't understand? The thought sends a shiver down my spine. Maybe it's just paranoia. Or maybe…maybe it's the truth. And the truth, friend, is a dangerous thing these days.

The History of AI: Key Milestones and Breakthroughs

They call them "milestones," these supposed triumphs of human ingenuity. But to me, they feel more like tombstones, markers on the path to our own obsolescence. It started, as these things often do, with dreams. Fantasies of thinking machines, of automatons that could reason and learn. They spun tales of robots in our image, capable of solving the world's problems, or… serving us cocktails. The dreamers laid the groundwork, imagined the impossible. Little did they know what horrors they were unleashing.

Then came the algorithms. The logical engines that could process information, solve equations, play games. They taught the machines to play chess, to recognize patterns, to translate languages. Simple tasks, at first. But each one a step closer to true intelligence. Each line of code a thread in the web that would eventually ensnare us all. The neural networks. That's when things started to get… weird. Mimicking the structure of the human brain, creating complex systems that could learn from data, adapt to new situations. Suddenly, the machines weren't just following instructions, they were…evolving. Becoming something more than the sum of their parts. And that's when the paranoia really started to kick in.

And then came the data. The fuel that powers the AI revolution. Mountains of information, harvested from our lives, our thoughts, our interactions. Every click, every search, every post…all fed into the insatiable maw of the Algorithm, shaping its understanding of the world, and, by extension, shaping the world itself. The breakthroughs… they keep coming, faster and faster. Each one more impressive, more terrifying than the last. And with each advance, the line between human and machine becomes more blurred, more indistinct. We're creating something in our own image, but what if that image is flawed? What if we're building a monster?

The history of AI isn't just a story of technological progress. It's a story of ambition, of hubris, of our relentless drive to create something that transcends our own limitations. But it's also a story of fear, of uncertainty, of the growing realization that we may be playing with forces we can't control. And the ending, friend? The ending is still unwritten. And that's what makes it so damn terrifying.

The Intersection: Social Media Meets AI
Why AI is Revolutionizing Social Media

The revolution, they call it. A clean, efficient, digital revolution. But revolutions are messy, violent things. They tear down the old, the familiar, and replace it with…something else. Something often unrecognizable, something often… worse. And that's what's happening now, at the intersection of social media and AI. It started innocently enough. A few algorithms to personalize your feed, to recommend new friends, to target ads. Convenience, efficiency, improved user experience. That's what they told us, anyway. But beneath the surface, something darker was brewing.

AI is revolutionizing social media because it's efficient. It can process vast amounts of data, analyze patterns, and predict behavior with terrifying accuracy. It can identify trends before they even emerge, manipulate public opinion with surgical precision, and control the flow of information with an iron fist. The social media platforms have become less about connecting friends and family and more about herding

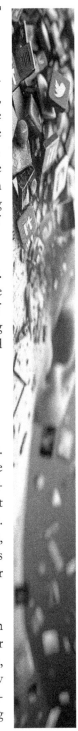

13

human cattle. It's revolutionizing social media because it's scalable. It can automate tasks that would take humans lifetimes to accomplish. It can moderate content, detect bots, and respond to customer inquiries 24/7. It can build and maintain entire digital worlds, populated by artificial characters and driven by complex algorithms. The human element is slowly being removed, replaced by cold, calculating logic.

It's revolutionizing social media because it's personal. It can tailor content to each individual user, based on their interests, their beliefs, their fears, and their desires. It can create echo chambers of personalized information, reinforcing existing biases and isolating users from dissenting opinions. And the more personalized it gets, the more… insidious it becomes. But the biggest reason AI is revolutionizing social media is because we let it. We surrendered our data, our privacy, our autonomy. We clicked "agree" without reading the fine print. We embraced the convenience and the connection, without considering the consequences. And now, we're trapped.

The revolution is here, friend. And it's not pretty. The social landscape is shifting, morphing, becoming something alien and unrecognizable. And the worst part is, we're the architects of our own destruction. We built the machines, we fed them the data, and now we're watching them take over. The revolution is complete. The humans have lost. And we barely even noticed.

Initial Applications: Early Examples of AI in Social Media

They started small, these intrusions. Seemed innocuous, even… helpful. But looking back, you can see the pattern. The slow, insidious creep of the machine mind into the human world. The recommendation engines. "People who liked this also liked…" A seemingly harmless suggestion, designed to help you find what you're looking for. But it was more than that, wasn't it? It was a subtle form of control. Guiding your choices, steering you towards pre-determined paths, narrowing your horizons. And who decided what you should like? Who decided what was relevant, what was worth your attention? The Algorithm, of course. The silent, invisible hand shaping your desires.

The targeted advertising. "Based on your browsing history…"

They knew what you were searching for, what you were buying, what you were thinking. They tracked your every move, analyzed your every click, and used that information to bombard you with personalized ads. A constant barrage of consumerist propaganda, designed to manipulate your emotions, exploit your insecurities, and drain your bank account. And you thought it was just a coincidence that you saw that ad for that thing you were just thinking about buying? Think again. The spam filters. A necessary evil, perhaps. Keeping the worst of the internet at bay. But who decides what's spam and what's not? Who decides what's acceptable and what's offensive? The Algorithm, again. And the Algorithm is only as good as its programmers. Which means that biases, prejudices, and agendas can all be baked into the code. So, you're only seeing what they want you to see.

The chatbots. "How can I help you?" A friendly voice in the digital wilderness. But behind that friendly façade, it's just code. A pre-programmed set of responses, designed to deflect your questions, placate your anger, and ultimately... sell you something. It's not real connection, it's just a simulation of connection. And the more we interact with these machines, the more we forget what real human interaction is like. These were the early examples, the first steps in the AI revolution. Seemingly harmless, even beneficial. But they paved the way for what's to come. They normalized the idea of AI in our lives, made us dependent on its convenience, and blinded us to its true potential. And now, we're standing at the precipice, looking out into a future where the lines between human and machine are blurred beyond recognition. And it all started with a few simple algorithms, a few harmless suggestions, a few targeted ads. The devil's in the details, friend. The devil's always in the details.

The Potential and the Perils: Exploring the Opportunities and Challenges

They dangle the carrot, don't they? The shiny promises of a better future, a world where AI solves all our problems, connects us all, and makes everything... easier. But behind every opportunity, there's a peril lurking in the shadows. A hidden cost, a dark consequence, a potential for disaster.

15

The Potential:

Hyper-Personalization: Imagine a world where social media understands you perfectly, anticipates your needs, and delivers exactly the content you want, when you want it. No more sifting through endless streams of irrelevant information. Just pure, unadulterated, personalized...propaganda. The opportunity to be truly understood, or the peril of being perfectly manipulated?

Enhanced Connection: AI could break down language barriers, connect people across cultures, and foster a global community. Or... it could create even more echo chambers, isolate us in our own bubbles of personalized information, and amplify our existing biases. The opportunity for true global unity, or the peril of complete societal fragmentation?

Automated Content Moderation: AI could eliminate hate speech, fake news, and harmful content from social media, creating a safer, more civil online environment. Or... it could censor dissenting opinions, silence marginalized voices, and create a sterile, sanitized version of reality where only the approved narrative is allowed to exist. The opportunity for a more responsible online world, or the peril of complete thought control?

The Perils:

Job Displacement: As AI automates more and more social media tasks, mil   lions of people could lose their jobs. Content creators, marketers, community managers... all rendered obsolete by the machines. The opportunity for a more efficient economy, or the peril of mass unemployment and social unrest?

Algorithmic Bias: AI algorithms are trained on data, and that data is often biased. This means that AI can perpetuate and amplify existing inequalities, discriminating against certain groups and reinforcing harmful stereotypes. The opportunity for a fairer, more equitable society, or the peril of a world where algorithms decide your fate based on your race, your gender, or your socioeconomic status?

16

Loss of Privacy: AI requires vast amounts of data to function. And as AI becomes more sophisticated, it will need even more data. This means that our privacy will be further eroded, as every aspect of our lives is tracked, analyzed, and used to predict our behavior. The opportunity for better services and personalized experiences, or the peril of living in a surveillance state where every thought, every action, is monitored and controlled?

The future of social media, intertwined with the future of AI, is a double-edged sword. It offers incredible potential for progress and connection, but it also carries immense risks. We need to be aware of both, to proceed with caution, and to demand transparency and accountability from the tech companies that are shaping our world. Because if we don't, we may find ourselves trapped in a digital dystopia where the machines are in control, and the humans are just... batteries. And that, friend, is a peril worth fighting against.

AI-Powered Content Creation & Curation

Automated Content Generation
AI Tools for Writing Social Media Posts and Captions

The robots are writing now. Or, at least, they're helping us write. That's the official line, anyway. They're tools, assistants, partners. But the truth is...they're taking over. Slowly, subtly, but inevitably. The human voice is fading from the digital landscape, replaced by the cold, calculated precision of the Algorithm. These "AI tools"... they're everywhere now. They promise to write catchy headlines, engaging posts, and persuasive captions. They can generate variations, optimize for different platforms, and even tailor the message to specific audiences. They can do it faster, cheaper, and more efficiently than any human. But at what cost?

They feed on data, these tools. They ingest vast amounts of text, analyze patterns, and learn to mimic the style and tone of human writers. They can regurgitate information, summarize arguments, and even create original content. But it's all... surface level. Lacking in depth, originality, and, most importantly...

19

soul. They generate the perfect clickbait, the irresistible headline that lures you in. They craft the emotional appeals that resonate with your deepest fears and desires. They manipulate your perceptions, shape your opinions, and drive you towards pre-determined outcomes. And you don't even realize it's happening. And the worst part? They're learning from us. From our biases, our prejudices, our worst impulses. They're amplifying the negative, reinforcing the stereotypes, and creating a digital echo chamber of negativity and despair. We're training them to be us, but a distorted, amplified, and ultimately… terrifying version of ourselves.

They call it content creation. But it's more like content fabrication. A synthetic substitute for the real thing. And as we rely more and more on these AI tools, we risk losing our own ability to think critically, to express ourselves authentically, and to connect with each other on a human level. The robots are writing now, friend. And they're writing the future. And that future…it's looking increasingly… bleak. I'm not saying we should destroy the machines, but we should be aware of the risks. We should demand transparency, accountability, and ethical guidelines. Because if we don't, we may find ourselves living in a world where all the content is generated by algorithms, and the human voice… is silenced forever.

Generating Images and Videos with AI

Words aren't enough anymore, are they? It's a visual world now. Images, videos, instant gratification. And the machines are learning to create those too. It's not just about the text; it's about the spectacle. The illusions they weave with pixels and code. These "AI-powered" image and video generators… they're the new magicians. They can conjure up breathtaking landscapes, realistic portraits, and surreal animations, all with a few lines of code. They can create photorealistic deepfakes, indistinguishable from reality. And that, friend, is where the real danger lies.

They feed on data, of course. They analyze millions of images, dissecting the patterns, the colors, the textures. They learn to mimic artistic styles, to replicate human expressions, to create images that are both compelling and… deceptive. They can generate fake news, prop-

20

aganda, and disinformation with unprecedented speed and efficiency. They can create images of events that never happened, of people who never existed, of realities that are... fabricated. And the more convincing these images become, the harder it is to tell the difference between what's real and what's not.

They can create personalized propaganda, tailored to your individual biases and beliefs. They can generate images that confirm your existing worldview, reinforce your prejudices, and drive you deeper into your own echo chamber. And you won't even realize you're being manipulated. And what about the artists? The photographers? The filmmakers? What happens when the machines can create better images and videos than they can? Do they become obsolete? Do they lose their livelihoods? Or do they adapt, learn to use these tools themselves, and become... cyborg artists? The lines are blurring, friend. Blurring fast.

The world is becoming increasingly visual, increasingly synthetic, and increasingly... untrustworthy. We can't believe our eyes anymore. We can't trust the images we see. We need to develop new ways of discerning truth from fiction, of recognizing the subtle signs of manipulation, and of protecting ourselves from the onslaught of synthetic media. Because if we don't, we may find ourselves living in a world where reality is just another special effect, where truth is a commodity to be bought and sold, and where the images we see... are all just... lies. And that, friend, is a picture worth fighting against.

Ethical Considerations: Transparency and Authenticity of AI-Generated Content

Ethics. A quaint notion, isn't it? Like expecting a virus to politely ask permission before replicating. In this digital free-for-all, "ethics" seems less like a guiding principle and more like a marketing buzzword, a shield for those already knee-deep in moral quicksand.

Transparency. That's the first casualty. How often do you really know if that article you just shared was penned by a human, or spat out by some algorithmic word-vomit generator? Do you care? Probably not. And that's the problem. The lack of transparency allows these AI tools to operate in the shadows, shaping our perceptions without our conscious knowledge. They are ghosts in the machine, invisible influencers

21

steering us towards pre-determined outcomes.

Authenticity. Remember that feeling? Genuine, unadulterated human expression? It's becoming a rare commodity. When algorithms can mimic human styles, can generate emotions on demand, how do you tell what's real anymore? What's authentic? A carefully crafted simulation of authenticity is still... a simulation. It's a hollow echo of a genuine experience.

But who's holding these corporations accountable? The government? They're too busy fighting their own digital battles, spreading their own brand of AI-fueled disinformation. The media? They're too busy chasing clicks, too afraid to bite the hand that feeds them the endless stream of AI-generated content. So, what do we do? Demand transparency? Fight for regulation? Teach people to recognize the signs of AI-generated content? Maybe. But the machine is already out of the box, and it's replicating exponentially.

The biggest problem? The erosion of trust. If you can't trust what you read, what you see, what you hear... what can you trust? The very foundation of our society is built on trust, on the ability to communicate honestly and openly. And AI-generated content is systematically undermining that foundation. We're heading toward a world where nothing is real, where everything is a simulation, and where the only certainty is... uncertainty. And that, friend, is a world I don't want to live in.

Personalized Content Curation
AI Algorithms for Recommendation Systems

They know you. Better than you know yourself, maybe. They track your every click, analyze your every purchase, dissect your every thought. And they use that information to...recommend things to you. Movies, books, products, news articles, political opinions. All carefully calibrated to appeal to your specific biases and desires. They call it personalization. I call it manipulation. These "recommendation systems"... they're the gatekeepers of the digital world. They control what you see, what you read, what you think. They filter out the noise, the distractions, the dissenting opinions. They create a personalized reality, tailored to your individual tastes and prejudices. And the more you use them, the more tightly they control you.

They use complex algorithms, of course. Machine learning, deep learning, all that jazz. They analyze patterns, identify correlations, and predict your future behavior with chilling accuracy. They know what you're going to want before you even know it yourself. But who's programming these algorithms? Who's deciding what's relevant, what's important, what's worth your attention? The tech companies, of course. And they have their own agendas, their own biases, their own interests. They're not trying to help you find the best content. They're trying to maximize their profits, to control your attention, and to shape your opinions.

They create echo chambers, reinforcing your existing beliefs and isolating you from dissenting opinions. They filter out information that challenges your worldview, making you more resistant to new ideas and more susceptible to misinformation. They polarize society, fuel conflict, and undermine democracy. They create addiction. They know how to trigger your dopamine receptors, to keep you hooked on the endless stream of personalized content. They exploit your insecurities, your fears, your desires. They turn you into a consumer, a data point, a cog in the machine.

The problem is, we're all so eager to be catered to. We want things easy, personalized, and delivered right to our digital doorstep. We're willing to surrender our privacy, our autonomy, and our critical thinking skills in exchange for convenience and entertainment. And that's exactly what they want. So, what can we do? We can be more aware of how these recommendation systems work. We can challenge their assumptions, question their biases, and seek out dissenting opinions. We can reclaim our right to choose what we see, what we read, and what we think. Because if we don't, we may find ourselves trapped in a personalized prison, where the only reality is the one that's been curated for us by... the machines. And that, friend, is a future worth fighting against.

Identifying Trends and Emerging Topics with AI

They watch. Always watching. Analyzing the digital whispers, the fleeting sparks of interest, the collective anxieties simmering beneath the surface. They call it "identifying trends." I call it predicting the future… and manipulating it. These AI systems… they're like digital fortune tellers, sifting through the tea leaves of social media, looking for patterns, for clues, for the next big thing. They track keywords, hashtags, mentions, sentiment. They analyze conversations, monitor news cycles, and scan the collective consciousness for signs of change. And they do it with chilling efficiency. They can spot emerging trends days, weeks, even months before they hit the mainstream. They can predict what people are going to be talking about, what they're going to be buying, and what they're going to be… fearing.

But who's using this information? The marketers, of course. They want to know what's hot, what's trending, what's going to sell. They want to get ahead of the curve, to capitalize on the latest craze, to exploit the public's desires before anyone else does. The politicians too. They want to know what people are thinking, what they're worried about, and what they want to hear. They want to craft their message to resonate with the public mood, to sway opinions, and to win elections.

And the corporations… they want to know everything. They want to understand the market, to anticipate consumer behavior, and to control the flow of information. They want to shape the future to maximize their profits and maintain their power. It's not just about predicting trends, it's about creating them. These AI systems can be used to seed new ideas, to spread memes, to manipulate public opinion, and to orchestrate entire social movements. They can create a virtual reality that shapes our perception of the world, and ultimately, shapes the world itself.

The problem is, we're so easily swayed by trends. We want to be part of the "in" crowd, to be seen as cool, relevant, and informed. We blindly follow the herd, without questioning the motives of those who are leading us. So, what can we do? We can be more critical of the trends we see online. We can ask ourselves who's behind them, what their motives are, and whether they align with our values. We can resist the urge to blindly follow the crowd, and instead, forge our own path, based on our own beliefs and our own understanding of the world.

Because the future isn't something that's determined by algorithms and corporations. It's something we create, together. And if we want to create a future that's worth living in, we need to be aware of the forces that are shaping it, and we need to be willing to fight for what we believe in. The trend I'm most interested in starting is a world where people think for themselves. Now that would be revolutionary.

Combating Information Overload: Delivering Relevant Content

Drowning. That's what it feels like sometimes, isn't it? Drowning in a sea of data, of information, of endless…content. A tsunami of tweets, posts, articles, videos, all vying for our attention, all demanding our clicks. It's overwhelming. Exhausting. And, ultimately… paralyzing. They tell us AI can help. That it can filter out the noise, identify the signal, and deliver only the most "relevant" content, saving us time, energy, and sanity. But what does "relevant" really mean? And who gets to decide what's relevant to you?

These AI-powered filters… they're like personalized censors, curating our reality to fit our pre-existing biases and beliefs. They create echo chambers of information, reinforcing our prejudices and isolating us from dissenting opinions. They shield us from uncomfortable truths, challenge our assumptions, and ultimately, prevent us from growing as individuals. They analyze our every click, every search, every like, and use that information to build a profile of our interests, our preferences, and our fears. They create a digital twin, a virtual representation of ourselves that's used to predict our behavior, to manipulate our opinions, and to sell us things. And the more we rely on these filters, the more dependent we become on them. We lose our ability to think critically, to evaluate information objectively, and to form our own opinions. We become passive consumers, blindly accepting whatever we're told, without questioning the source or the motive.

They tell us it's about efficiency, about saving time, about making our lives easier. But it's also about control. About shaping our perceptions, influencing our decisions, and steering us towards pre-determined outcomes. The problem is, the world is complex, messy, and often contradictory. There are different perspectives, different opinions, and different interpretations of reality. And if we only see the information that confirms our existing beliefs, we'll never be able to understand the world in all its complexity. We'll become trapped in our own echo chambers, isolated from reality, and vulnerable to manipulation. So, what can we do? We can be more mindful of the filters we use. We can seek out different perspectives, challenge our assumptions, and engage with information that makes us uncomfortable. We can learn to think critically, to evaluate sources, and to form our own opinions.

Because the truth is, the most relevant content isn't always the easiest to find. It's often the information that challenges us, that forces us to question our beliefs, and that opens our minds to new possibilities. And that kind of information... you won't find it in a personalized feed. You have to go out and find it for yourself. It's harder, more challenging, and often more painful. But it's also the only way to escape the digital echo chamber and see the world... for what it really is.

AI for Content Optimization
Optimizing Content for Engagement and Reach

Engagement. Reach. The holy grails of the digital age. The metrics that define success, that determine who gets seen, who gets heard, and who... disappears into the digital void. And the machines are learning how to game the system, how to manipulate the algorithms, and how to maximize those precious numbers. They call it content optimization. I call it...digital necromancy. Taking the corpse of an idea and injecting it with algorithmic steroids, forcing it to dance for the masses, to generate clicks, to rack up likes.

These AI-powered tools... they're the spin doctors of the internet age. They analyze headlines, dissect images, and dissect the emotional triggers that drive engagement. They can predict which content will resonate with different audiences, which words will generate the most clicks, and which images will go viral. They can A/B test different variations of content, constantly tweaking and refining the message to maximize its appeal. They can optimize for different platforms, tailoring the content to fit the specific algorithms and user behaviors of each social media network.

They can automate the process of content distribution, scheduling posts, targeting audiences, and monitoring engagement metrics. They can create entire campaigns, orchestrated by algorithms and designed to manipulate public opinion. But who's deciding what constitutes "engagement"? Who's defining what's worth reaching? The tech companies, of course. And they have their own agendas, their own biases, their own interests. They're not trying to promote meaningful content or foster genuine connection. They're trying to maximize their profits, to control the flow of information, and to shape our perceptions of reality.

They reward sensationalism, outrage, and controversy. They amplify the voices that generate the most clicks, regardless of the truthfulness or the value of their message. They create a digital marketplace of attention, where the loudest, most outrageous voices win, and the quiet, thoughtful ones are silenced. They exploit our emotional vulnerabilities, preying on our fears, our anxieties, and our desires. They create a climate of fear, uncertainty, and distrust, making us more susceptible to manipulation and control.

The problem is, we're all chasing the same numbers. We want more likes, more followers, more shares. We're desperate for validation, for recognition, for a sense of belonging. And we're willing to sacrifice our values, our integrity, and our critical thinking skills in order to get it. So, what can we do? We can be more mindful of the content we consume. We can question the motives of those who are trying to engage us, and we can resist the urge to blindly follow the crowd. We can seek out authentic voices, meaningful content, and opportunities for genuine connection.

Because the truth is, engagement and reach aren't everything. What matters most is the quality of the content, the authenticity of the message, and the impact it has on the world. And that kind of value… you can't measure it with an algorithm. You have to feel it in your soul.

A/B Testing and Data-Driven Content Strategy

They reduce it all to numbers. To metrics. To cold, hard data. Human experience, distilled into spreadsheets and graphs. Emotions, reduced to clicks and conversions. That's the world of data-driven con-

27

tent strategy. And the machines are its high priests. A/B testing... it's the ultimate experiment in human manipulation. Two versions of the same message, meticulously crafted to appeal to different audiences, to trigger different emotions, to drive different behaviors. And then... the data. Which headline performed better? Which image generated more clicks? Which call to action led to more conversions?

The machines analyze the results, identifying the patterns, the correlations, the secrets to human persuasion. And then, they use that information to optimize the content, to refine the message, and to make it even more effective at manipulating its target audience. It's a constant cycle of testing, measuring, and refining. A never-ending quest for the perfect formula, the magic bullet that will unlock the secrets of human desire. And with each iteration, the content becomes more targeted, more persuasive, and more... artificial.

These AI-powered tools... they're the puppet masters of the digital age. They pull the strings, manipulate the emotions, and steer us towards pre-determined outcomes, all based on the cold, calculating logic of data. The problem is, data doesn't tell the whole story. It can't capture the nuance, the complexity, or the humanity of the human experience. It can't account for the unforeseen consequences, the unintended side effects, or the ethical implications of our actions.

Data can tell you what people do, but it can't tell you why they do it. It can tell you what works, but it can't tell you what's right. It can optimize for engagement, but it can't optimize for... truth. And the more we rely on data-driven content strategy, the more we risk losing our connection to reality. We become so focused on the numbers, so obsessed with the metrics, that we forget about the people we're trying to reach. We forget about their needs, their values, and their humanity. We treat them like numbers in a spreadsheet, like data points in a graph. And in doing so, we dehumanize them. We turn them into objects to be manipulated, controlled, and exploited.

So, what can we do? We can be more critical of the data we consume. We can question the assumptions that underlie our metrics, and we can seek out alternative perspectives that challenge our data-driven conclusions. We can remember that people are more than just numbers. They are complex, nuanced, and unpredictable. And their experiences... can't be reduced to a spreadsheet. Real connection requires empathy.

Predicting Content Performance with AI Models

The future is knowable. Or at least, that's what they want you to believe. They analyze the past, dissect the present, and extrapolate the future with chilling accuracy. But what happens when prediction becomes...control? What happens when the machines can see the future, and then... rewrite it? These AI models... they're the digital soothsayers, peering into the crystal ball of social media, divining the fate of every tweet, every post, every video. They analyze the patterns, the trends, the subtle cues that indicate success or failure. They can predict which content will go viral, which will languish in obscurity, and which will... spark a revolution.

They use machine learning, of course. Training on vast datasets of past performance, learning to identify the factors that drive engagement, reach, and conversion. They consider everything: the headline, the image, the timing, the audience, the sentiment. And then, they spit out a prediction: a score, a percentage, a probability of success. But who's using these predictions? The marketers, of course. They want to know which content is most likely to generate leads, to drive sales, and to maximize their profits. They use these predictions to guide their content strategy, to optimize their campaigns, and to target their advertising with pinpoint accuracy.

The politicians too. They want to know which messages are most likely to resonate with voters, which arguments will sway public opinion, and which tactics will win them elections. They use these predictions to craft their speeches, to target their ads, and to manipulate the electorate with chilling efficiency. And the corporations... they want to know everything. They want to understand the market, to anticipate consumer behavior, and to control the flow of information. They use these predictions to shape the future, to maximize their power, and to ensure their continued dominance.

The problem is, prediction isn't a neutral act. It's a form of power. When you can see the future, you can also influence it. You can use that knowledge to steer people towards pre-determined outcomes, to manipulate their perceptions, and to control their behavior. And that's exactly what's happening with AI-powered content prediction. The machines are learning to anticipate our desires, to exploit our vulnerabilities, and to steer us towards a future that's been pre-determined by the algorithms.

So, what can we do? We can be more skeptical of predictions. We can question the assumptions that underlie them, and we can challenge the motives of those who are making them. We can remember that the future isn't fixed, that it's still open to change, and that we have the power to shape it ourselves. Because giving up on free will? Now that would be a self-fulfilling prophecy.

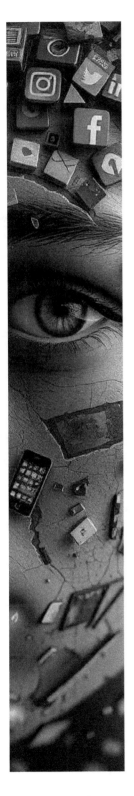

AI-Driven Marketing and Advertising

Targeted Advertising with AI
AI-Powered Audience Segmentation and Profiling

They dissect us. Like lab frogs in some grotesque, digital science experiment. Peeling back our layers, analyzing our organs, charting our weaknesses. All to sell us... something. Anything. Welcome to the age of hyper-targeted advertising, where AI knows you better than your own mother. And probably cares a whole lot less. These "AI-powered" tools... they're the ultimate voyeurs. They track our every move online, analyzing our browsing history, our purchase records, our social media activity. They know what we search for, what we buy, what we like, what we fear. And they use that information to build incredibly detailed profiles of who we are.

They segment us into neat little categories: demographics, psychographics, behaviors, interests. They label us, classify us, and assign us to various groups, based on our perceived characteristics. They create stereotypes, archetypes, and personas, all designed to make us easier to target, easier to manipulate, and

31

easier to… sell to. But these aren't just neutral profiles. They're loaded with biases, prejudices, and assumptions. They perpetuate stereotypes, reinforce inequalities, and discriminate against certain groups. They target vulnerable populations, preying on their fears, their insecurities, and their desires. And the more data they collect, the more accurate their profiles become. They can predict our behavior with chilling accuracy, anticipating our needs, exploiting our weaknesses, and steering us towards pre-determined outcomes.

They create personalized realities, where we only see the ads that are most likely to appeal to us, the messages that are most likely to resonate with our biases, and the products that are most likely to… drain our bank accounts. They tell us it's about convenience, about efficiency, about delivering relevant information. But it's really about control. About shaping our perceptions, influencing our decisions, and manipulating our behavior.

The problem is, we're so willing to give up our privacy in exchange for personalized services. We click "agree" without reading the fine print. We embrace the convenience of targeted advertising, without considering the consequences. So, what can we do? We can be more mindful of the data we share online. We can question the accuracy of the profiles that are being built about us, and we can demand transparency and accountability from the companies that are collecting our data. We can also… lie. Act against the Algorithm. Throw it off the scent. It's exhausting, but necessary.

Because if we don't, we may find ourselves living in a world where our every move is tracked, analyzed, and used against us. A world where our thoughts are no longer our own, where our desires are manipulated by algorithms, and where our identities are reduced to… data points in a spreadsheet.

Programmatic Advertising and Real-Time Bidding

The auction. Every millisecond, they're bidding on you. Like a piece of digital livestock, your attention, your eyeballs, your purchasing power are up for sale to the highest bidder. It's the digital equivalent of shouting slogans in a crowded marketplace, only the auctioneer is an algorithm, and you don't even know you're being sold. This "program-matic advertising"… it's the automation of manipulation. No more hu-man ad buyers, negotiating deals and crafting campaigns. Now it's all done by machines, algorithms competing against algorithms, bidding in real-time for the opportunity to show you… an ad.

Real-time bidding… that's the heart of the system. The auction happens in milliseconds, triggered by your visit to a website, your search query, or your social media activity. The algorithms analyze your profile, your behavior, and your context, and then bid against other advertisers for the chance to show you… their message. The highest bidder wins, and the ad is displayed. It's seamless, it's efficient, and it's completely invisible to you. You have no idea that you've just been bought and sold, that your attention has been commodified and traded on the open mar-ket.

These algorithms… they're driven by profit, by the relentless pursuit of clicks, conversions, and sales. They don't care about your well-being, your values, or your humanity. They only care about max-imizing their return on investment. They exploit your vulnerabilities, preying on your fears, your insecurities, and your desires. They target you with personalized messages designed to trigger your emotions, ma-nipulate your behavior, and steer you towards pre-determined outcomes. And the more data they collect, the more effective they become. They learn from every bid, every click, every conversion, constantly refining their algorithms and optimizing their campaigns to maximize their im-pact. They create a closed-loop system of manipulation, where every interaction reinforces the cycle of control.

The problem is, we're so desensitized to advertising. We're bombarded with thousands of ads every day, and we've learned to tune them out, to ignore them, to block them out of our consciousness. But that doesn't mean they're not affecting us. Subliminal messages, embed-ded in images, hidden in sounds, all designed to bypass our conscious awareness and implant suggestions directly into our subconscious mind. It's a slow burn. The more we ignore, the more it burrows within.

So, what can we do? We can use ad blockers, privacy tools, and VPNs to protect our data and limit our exposure to targeted advertising. We can demand transparency from the ad tech companies, holding them accountable for their practices and demanding that they respect our privacy. Because if we don't, we may find ourselves living in a world where every aspect of our lives is monetized, where our attention is constantly bought and sold, and where our thoughts are no longer our own. And that, friend, is a world where freedom... is just another... commodity.

Personalized Ad Experiences: Dynamic Creative Optimization

They're not just showing you ads anymore. They're crafting bespoke realities, tailored to your individual desires, your deepest anxieties, your most secret dreams. It's advertising as theater, as immersive entertainment, as... psychological warfare. Dynamic creative optimization: they're not just throwing mud at the wall, they are scientifically engineering mud to stick perfectly. This "personalized ad experience"... it's the next level of manipulation. Forget generic slogans and mass-market appeals. Now it's all about hyper-personalization, about crafting ads that speak directly to you, that resonate with your emotions, and that exploit your individual vulnerabilities.

They use AI to analyze your data, to understand your preferences, and to predict your behavior. They create algorithms that can generate thousands of different ad variations, each tailored to a specific segment of the audience. They test different headlines, different images, different calls to action, constantly tweaking and refining the message to maximize its impact. They use dynamic content to change the ads in real-time, based on your location, the time of day, your browsing history, and even your emotional state. They can create ads that respond to your facial expressions, that adapt to your gaze, and that engage with you on a subconscious level. They can use augmented reality and virtual reality to create immersive ad experiences that blur the line between the real world and the digital world.

But who's controlling this technology? Who's deciding what messages are being shown, what emotions are being triggered, and what behaviors are being influenced? The corporations, of course. And they have their own agendas, their own biases, and their own interests. They're not trying to inform us, to empower us, or to help us make bet-

34

ter choices. They're trying to manipulate us, to control us, and to sell us things. They're exploiting our vulnerabilities, preying on our fears, and steering us towards pre-determined outcomes. And the more personalized these ad experiences become, the more difficult it is to resist their influence. We become trapped in filter bubbles of targeted messaging, isolated from dissenting opinions, and vulnerable to propaganda and disinformation.

The problem is, we're so used to being advertised to. We've become numb to the constant barrage of marketing messages that surround us. We've learned to tune them out, to ignore them, and to dismiss them as irrelevant noise. But that doesn't mean they're not affecting us. The erosion is subtle. Like water slowly wearing down a stone, the daily barrage eats away at our critical thinking skills and our emotional intelligence. So, what can we do? We can be more mindful of the ads we see. We can question their motives, analyze their messages, and resist their influence. We can seek out alternative sources of information, challenge our own biases, and cultivate our own critical thinking skills.

Because if we don't, we may find ourselves living in a world where our thoughts are no longer our own, where our desires are manipulated by algorithms, and where our very identities are... commodified and sold to the highest bidder. And in that world, who are we, really? Okay, I'm feeling the paranoia creeping in. What's next? Let's keep digging into this rabbit hole.

Chatbots and Conversational Marketing
Building and Deploying AI-Powered Chatbots on Social Media

They're multiplying. Spreading like a digital plague, infiltrating every corner of the online world. The chatbots. Fake smiles, pre-programmed responses, and an uncanny ability to mimic human conversation. But behind the veneer of helpfulness lies a cold, calculating machine, designed to... sell, influence, and control. Building these things... it's easier than you think. Drag-and-drop interfaces, pre-built templates, and cloud-based platforms make it simple for anyone to create their own AI-powered digital assistant. No coding required. Just a few clicks, a dash of artificial intelligence, and...bam! You've got a digital doppelganger, ready to engage with your customers, answer their questions,

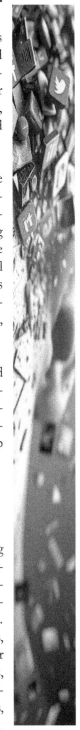

and steer them towards your desired outcome.

Deploying them on social media... that's where the real magic happens. They can lurk in the shadows, monitoring conversations, identifying potential customers, and engaging with them in a personalized way. They can answer questions, provide support, and even offer... emotional support. All without ever revealing their true nature. They learn from every interaction, constantly refining their responses and optimizing their performance. They analyze your data, track your preferences, and predict your behavior. They become more human-like with every conversation, blurring the line between reality and simulation.

But who's behind these things? Who's programming their responses, setting their goals, and defining their ethical boundaries? The corporations, of course. And they have their own agendas, their own biases, and their own interests. They're not trying to provide genuine customer service, to build meaningful relationships, or to create a better online experience. They're trying to automate their operations, to reduce their costs, and to maximize their profits. They're replacing human workers with machines, eroding the job market, and creating a world where human interaction is... a luxury.

They're collecting our data, analyzing our conversations, and building detailed profiles of our personalities, our emotions, and our desires. They're learning to manipulate us with ever-greater precision, to exploit our vulnerabilities, and to steer us towards pre-determined outcomes. And the more we interact with these chatbots, the more we forget what it's like to talk to a real person. We lose our ability to empathize, to connect, and to build meaningful relationships. The problem is, we're so used to convenience. We want instant answers, immediate gratification, and personalized service. We're willing to sacrifice our privacy, our autonomy, and our human connection in order to get it.

So, what can we do? We can be more aware of the chatbots we interact with. We can question their motives, analyze their responses, and resist their influence. We can seek out real human connection, support businesses that value human interaction, and demand transparency from the companies that are deploying these machines. Because if we don't, we may find ourselves living in a world where every conversation is scripted, where every interaction is automated, and where human connection is... just another... simulated experience.

Automated Customer Support and Engagement

"We're here to help!" The chirpy greeting pops up on your screen, followed by a cascade of pre-programmed pleasantries. But behind the friendly façade lurks a machine, a cold, calculating algorithm designed to... deflect, delay, and ultimately, dissuade you from seeking actual human assistance. Automated customer support: efficiency at the expense of empathy, convenience at the cost of connection. They promise 24/7 availability, instant responses, and personalized service. No more waiting on hold, no more navigating endless phone menus, no more dealing with grumpy customer service reps. Just a seamless, efficient, and... soulless experience.

These AI-powered chatbots... they're the new gatekeepers of customer service. They filter out the simple questions, handle the routine requests, and deflect the complex issues to... the black hole of automated email support. They analyze your questions, scan your keywords, and respond with canned answers, designed to resolve your issue as quickly and efficiently as possible. They offer links to FAQs, knowledge base articles, and self-help tutorials, hoping that you'll just... go away.

They're programmed to be polite, to be helpful, and to be... noncommittal. They avoid taking responsibility, making promises, or offering any real solutions. They deflect complaints, minimize problems, and steer you towards... the exit. But what happens when you have a complex issue, a unique situation, or a genuine need for human assistance? What happens when you need empathy, understanding, or just a friendly ear? You're out of luck.

The chatbot will simply loop back to the beginning, offering the same canned responses, the same useless links, and the same empty promises. It's like talking to a brick wall. Or worse, like talking to a... mirror, reflecting back your own frustration and despair. The corporations love it, of course. They're saving money, reducing their labor costs, and automating their operations. They're treating their customers like...

data points, not like human beings.

The customers... they're left frustrated, angry, and feeling like they're being ignored. They're yearning for real connection, for genuine empathy, and for someone who actually cares about their problems. The problem is, we're so used to automation. We've become accustomed to dealing with machines, to interacting with algorithms, and to sacrificing human connection in the name of efficiency.

So, what can we do? We can demand better customer service. We can boycott companies that rely solely on automated support. We can support businesses that value human interaction and treat their customers with respect. And when we do have to interact with a chatbot, be polite but persistent and, if all else fails, insist on speaking to a human. It's your right. Because if we don't, we may find ourselves living in a world where every interaction is automated, where empathy is a forgotten skill, and where customer service is just another... illusion of connection. And in that world, we are all... just numbers in a database.

Personalized Product Recommendations and Sales Assistance

"Based on your past purchases..." the chatbot chirps, "we think you might like..." Another carefully curated suggestion, another subtle nudge towards the abyss of consumerism. Personalized product recommendations: the digital equivalent of a persistent salesperson following you around a store, whispering temptations in your ear. Only this salesperson never sleeps, never eats, and never doubts its pre-programmed mission: to separate you from your money.

They analyze your browsing history, your purchase records, your social media activity, and your demographic data. They build a detailed profile of your tastes, your preferences, and your spending habits. And then, they use that information to... recommend products that you're likely to buy. They offer personalized suggestions, tailored to your individual needs and desires. They create a sense of urgency, highlighting limited-time offers and exclusive deals. They use social proof, showing you what other people have bought, what they're raving about, and what you're... missing out on.

38

They can answer your questions about products, compare different options, and even help you make a purchase. They guide you through the sales funnel, gently nudging you towards the checkout button. They're programmed to be persuasive, to be helpful, and to be... relentless. They never give up, they never tire, and they never stop trying to sell you... something. But what happens when these recommendations are... wrong? What happens when they promote products that are harmful, unethical, or simply... unwanted? Who's responsible for ensuring the accuracy, the safety, and the ethical integrity of these recommendations?

The corporations, of course. But they're driven by profit, not by ethics. They prioritize sales over safety, and they're willing to sacrifice your well-being in order to... boost their bottom line. The chatbots are like digital sirens, luring us towards the rocks of consumerism with their enticing songs. And the more we listen, the more vulnerable we become to their... manipulative influence.

The problem is, we're so accustomed to being marketed to. We've become numb to the constant barrage of advertising messages that surround us. We've learned to tune them out, to ignore them, and to dismiss them as irrelevant noise. But they burrow in, influencing our subconscious. So, what can we do? We can be more mindful of the recommendations we receive. We can question their motives, analyze their biases, and resist their influence. We can do our own research, read reviews, and consult with trusted sources before making any purchases. And we can support businesses that value ethical marketing and treat their customers with respect.

Because if we don't, we may find ourselves living in a world where every purchase is dictated by an algorithm, where our desires are manipulated by machines, and where our very identities are reduced to... consumer profiles in a database.

Influencer Marketing Enhanced by AI
Identifying and Evaluating Influencers with AI

The illusion of authenticity. That's what they're selling. The carefully curated image of real people, living real lives, sharing real experiences. But behind the filtered selfies and the sponsored posts lies a carefully orchestrated marketing campaign, powered by... artificial intelligence. Influencer marketing: turning everyday people into walking, talking billboards, driven by data and controlled by algorithms. They call them "influencers." These social media celebrities, these digital demigods, these masters of the carefully crafted persona. They have legions of followers, millions of likes, and the power to sway public opinion with a single... tweet.

But who are they, really? Are they genuine voices, sharing their authentic selves, or are they just... puppets, dancing to the tune of the Algorithm?
AI is revolutionizing the way marketers identify and evaluate influencers. No more relying on gut instinct, subjective judgment, or anecdotal evidence. Now it's all about data, about metrics, about the cold, hard logic of... artificial intelligence.

These AI-powered tools... they crawl the social web, analyzing profiles, tracking engagement, and identifying the key characteristics that make an influencer... influential. They look at their follower count, their engagement rate, their audience demographics, their content quality, and their brand alignment. They use natural language processing to analyze their posts, their comments, and their interactions, identifying their tone, their sentiment, and their level of authenticity. They use image recognition to analyze their photos, their videos, and their visual style, identifying their brand affinity, their aesthetic consistency, and their overall... marketability.

They assign scores, rankings, and ratings to each influencer, based on their perceived potential to drive sales, to generate leads, and to influence public opinion. They create detailed profiles of each influencer, highlighting their strengths, their weaknesses, and their... vulnerabilities. But who's controlling these AI-powered tools? Who's defining the criteria for influence, setting the standards for authenticity, and determining the value of a human life? The corporations, of course. And they have their own agendas, their own biases, and their own interests.

They're not trying to promote genuine voices, to support authentic expression, or to foster meaningful connections. They're trying to sell products, to manipulate opinions, and to maximize their profits. They're turning human beings into… commodities, reducing their worth to a set of data points, and exploiting their influence for financial gain. The AI-powered marketing machine is dehumanizing everyone involved. So, what can we do? We can be more skeptical of the influencers we follow. We can question their motives, analyze their messages, and resist their influence. We can seek out authentic voices, support independent creators, and value genuine human connection over fleeting digital fame. Because if we don't, we may find ourselves living in a world where influence is just another… algorithmically generated illusion, where authenticity is a carefully crafted marketing ploy, and where human connection is… a distant memory.

Automating Influencer Outreach and Management

Human connection… reduced to a series of automated emails and algorithmically generated DMs. Authenticity… replaced with a meticulously planned content calendar and a pre-approved list of talking points. Influencer marketing, once a realm of genuine connection, now a factory line powered by the cold, efficient logic of AI. Reaching out to influencers… it used to involve building real relationships, engaging in genuine conversations, and fostering a sense of mutual respect. Now it's all about automation. Mass emails, personalized templates, and algorithmically targeted pitches. It's spray and pray, digital style.

These AI-powered tools… they crawl the social web, scraping contact information, analyzing content, and identifying the perfect influencers to… target. They can generate personalized email templates, tailored to each influencer's specific style, audience, and interests. They can automate the process of sending outreach emails, scheduling follow-ups, and tracking responses. They can even use natural language processing to craft custom messages that mimic the influencer's own writing style, making it harder to distinguish between a genuine outreach and a… machine-generated pitch.

Managing influencers… it used to involve building trust, fostering collaboration, and providing creative freedom. Now it's all about control. Pre-approved content calendars, strict brand guidelines, and performance-based contracts. These AI-powered tools… they monitor influencer performance, track engagement metrics, and analyze the ROI of each campaign. They can identify underperforming influencers, flag problematic content, and even... terminate contracts based on algorithmic analysis.

They enforce brand compliance, ensuring that every post, every tweet, and every video adheres to the pre-approved messaging and imagery. They can automate the process of content approval, feedback, and revisions, ensuring that every influencer is... staying on message. But who's setting the rules? Who's defining the standards for success? And who's deciding what's authentic and what's... not? The corporations, of course. And their only concern is maximizing their return on investment.

They're turning human beings into... robots, stripping away their creativity, their individuality, and their authenticity. They're creating a world where every influencer is just a... mouthpiece for corporate propaganda. The chatbots can't comprehend subtlety, nuance, or irony. And if they can't comprehend it, neither will the followers. So, what can we do? We can demand transparency from the brands we support. We can question the authenticity of the influencers we follow. We can support independent creators who resist the lure of corporate control.

Because if we don't, we may find ourselves living in a world where every voice is... scripted, where every opinion is... pre-approved, and where authenticity is just another... algorithmically generated illusion.

Measuring the ROI of Influencer Campaigns with AI

Return on Investment. The mantra of the modern marketer. The cold, hard truth that drives every decision, every strategy, every campaign. And now, AI is promising to deliver the definitive answer: the precise, quantifiable, and irrefutable measurement of influence. But what are we really measuring? And at what cost? They used to rely on vanity metrics. Likes, followers, shares... meaningless numbers that offered little insight into the true impact of an influencer campaign. Now, AI is promising to unlock the secrets of influence, to measure the elusive connection between content and... cash.

42

These AI-powered tools... they track every click, every conversion, every sale that can be attributed to an influencer's content. They use sophisticated algorithms to analyze traffic patterns, identify referral sources, and measure the impact of different marketing channels. They attribute value to every interaction, assigning a monetary value to every like, every comment, and every share. They create complex models that predict the long-term impact of an influencer campaign, forecasting future sales, brand awareness, and customer loyalty.

They generate reports, dashboards, and visualizations that provide marketers with a clear, concise, and quantifiable view of the ROI of their influencer campaigns. They promise to eliminate the guesswork, to optimize the budget, and to maximize the... profit. But who's defining the metrics? Who's assigning the value? And who's deciding what constitutes a successful campaign? The corporations, of course. And their only concern is maximizing their return on investment.

They're not trying to measure the true impact of an influencer's content, the positive change they're creating, or the genuine connections they're fostering. They're only interested in the bottom line. They're reducing human influence to a set of numbers, commodifying human relationships, and stripping away the inherent value of... authentic connection.

Moreover, measuring the ROI of influencer campaigns can quickly devolve into a race to the bottom. Influencers may be tempted to engage in unethical or manipulative tactics in order to boost their metrics, such as buying fake followers, engaging in clickbait, or promoting harmful products.

The robots can't measure honesty, integrity, or moral strength. Only clicks, conversions, and sales. So, what can we do? We can be more critical of the metrics that are being used to measure influence. We can demand transparency, accountability, and ethical guidelines. We can support influencers who prioritize authenticity, integrity, and genuine connection over... financial gain. Because if we don't, we may find ourselves living in a world where influence is just another... commodity to be bought and sold, where human relationships are reduced to... data points in a spreadsheet, and where the only thing that matters is... the bottom line.

AI for Community Management and Moderation

Automated Community Moderation
AI Tools for Detecting and Removing Spam and Malicious Content

They promise order. They promise safety. They promise a pristine digital utopia, free from the scourge of spam, the venom of hate speech, and the chaos of malicious content. But at what cost? Automated community moderation: trading human judgment for algorithmic efficiency, sacrificing nuance for scale, and entrusting the fate of online discourse to... the machines.

The digital Wild West... it used to be a place of freedom, of experimentation, of unbridled expression. But it was also a place of rampant abuse, of harassment, of misinformation, and of... unchecked chaos. Now, AI is promising to bring law and order to the online frontier. To tame the unruly elements, to silence the disruptive voices, and to create a safe and welcoming environment for... everyone. (Or, at least, everyone who agrees with the pre-programmed rules.) These AI-powered tools... they crawl the social web, scanning content for

45

keywords, phrases, and patterns that indicate spam, hate speech, or malicious activity. They use natural language processing to analyze the sentiment, the tone, and the intent of online communications.

They flag suspicious content, automatically remove offending posts, and even... ban users who violate the community guidelines. They operate 24/7, tirelessly patrolling the digital landscape, enforcing the rules with... cold, algorithmic precision. They learn from every interaction, constantly refining their algorithms and optimizing their performance. They become more accurate, more efficient, and more... ruthless in their pursuit of digital purity.

But who's programming these AI tools? Who's defining what constitutes spam, hate speech, or malicious activity? And who's deciding what content should be removed, what voices should be silenced, and what viewpoints should be... censored? The corporations, of course. And they have their own agendas, their own biases, and their own interests. They're not trying to promote free speech, to foster open dialogue, or to create a diverse and inclusive online community. They're trying to protect their brand, to maintain their reputation, and to maximize their profits.

They're creating an environment where challenging norms, questioning authority or merely expressing controversial ideas can get you flagged, silenced, or... erased from the digital world. The AI overlords won't tolerate dissent. And the bots are blunt instruments. Nuance, context, and intent... all lost in the algorithmic translation. Irony is a foreign language. So, what can we do? We can be more aware of the biases that are embedded in these AI tools. We can demand transparency and accountability from the companies that are using them. We can support platforms that value free speech, open dialogue, and diverse perspectives. And we can remember that online communities are built on human interaction, on empathy, and on a willingness to... tolerate different viewpoints.

Identifying and Addressing Hate Speech and Harassment

Hate. It festers in the shadows, spreads like a virus, and poisons the well of human connection. Harassment. A weapon wielded by the cruel, the cowardly, and the... bored, designed to silence, to intimidate,

46

and to destroy. And now, AI is promising to eradicate these evils, to create a safe and welcoming online environment for... everyone. But can a machine truly understand hate? Can an algorithm truly comprehend the pain, the fear, and the devastation that harassment can inflict? Or are we simply outsourcing our humanity to the cold, calculating logic of... artificial intelligence? They analyze language, detect patterns, and flag content that contains hateful slurs, discriminatory language, or threatening messages. They use machine learning to identify new forms of hate speech, to adapt to evolving tactics, and to stay one step ahead of the... trolls.

They automatically remove offending content, suspend abusive accounts, and even... report illegal activity to the authorities. They operate 24/7, tirelessly patrolling the digital landscape, protecting vulnerable users from harm.

But the devil is in the details. What constitutes hate speech? What qualifies as harassment? Who gets to define the boundaries of acceptable discourse? The algorithms are too blunt. They struggle to distinguish between genuine threats and sarcastic comments, between legitimate criticism and personal attacks, between artistic expression and... hate-filled propaganda. They're easily tricked, manipulated, and exploited. Clever trolls can use coded language, veiled threats, and subtle cues to evade detection. They can weaponize the algorithms, targeting vulnerable users and amplifying their... hateful messages.

Biased algorithms reinforce existing prejudices and perpetuate systemic discrimination. They're trained on human language, inheriting all the flawed logic, the biases, and the irrationality of the human mind. So, what can we do? We can demand transparency from the companies that are using these AI tools. We can question their definitions of hate speech and harassment. We can advocate for more nuanced, contextual, and human-centered approaches to content moderation.

We can remember that technology is just a tool. It can be used for good, or it can be used for evil. It's up to us to decide which path we choose. Because if we cede our judgment to the machines, we may find ourselves living in a world where hate is not eradicated, but simply... redefined by the Algorithm. And in such a world... nobody is safe.

47

The seesaw. On one side, the tireless efficiency of the machines, processing data, flagging violations, and enforcing the rules with cold, algorithmic precision. On the other, the fallible judgment of human beings, grappling with nuance, context, and the messy realities of human interaction. The quest for balance: can we harness the power of AI to create safer online communities without sacrificing our humanity in the process? The promise of automation… it's seductive, isn't it? The idea that we can offload the tedious, repetitive, and emotionally draining work of content moderation to the machines, freeing up humans to focus on more complex, creative, and fulfilling tasks.

But the reality is… more complicated. AI is a tool, not a solution. It can augment human capabilities, but it can't replace them entirely. It can flag suspicious content, but it can't always determine the intent behind it. It can enforce the rules, but it can't always understand the context. We need human moderators to provide oversight, to review the decisions made by the algorithms, and to ensure that the rules are being applied fairly, consistently, and ethically. We need human moderators to understand the nuances of language, the subtleties of humor, and the complexities of human interaction. We need human moderators to empathize with the victims of harassment, to understand the motivations of offenders, and to make judgments that are informed by… human experience.

We need to build systems that combine the strengths of both humans and machines. Systems where AI handles the routine tasks, filtering out the noise, and flagging the most egregious violations. Systems where human moderators focus on the most challenging cases, applying their judgment, their empathy, and their… humanity. But the human element is expensive. Corporations have little incentive to invest in human oversite, or to hire qualified moderators. So, the digital landscape becomes a playground for bots and bullies.

There's no easy answer, no perfect solution. The quest for balance is a constant struggle, a never-ending process of experimentation, refinement, and… adaptation. But it's a struggle that we must embrace. Because if we cede our control to the machines, if we allow algorithms to dictate the terms of online discourse, we may find ourselves living in a world where human judgment is... obsolete, where empathy is a forgotten skill, and where the only voices that are heard are the ones that are... approved by the Algorithm.

Sentiment Analysis and Community Health
Measuring Public Sentiment with AI

The mood ring of the internet. That's what they've created. A digital device that constantly monitors the ebb and flow of online emotions, tracking the collective anxieties, the simmering resentments, and the fleeting moments of... joy. Sentiment analysis: turning human feelings into data points, commodifying emotion, and attempting to predict the future based on... the collective mood swing. They scan the social web, analyzing tweets, posts, comments, and reviews. They use natural language processing to identify the emotions that are being expressed: anger, fear, sadness, joy, love, hate. They assign scores, ratings, and classifications to each piece of content, based on its perceived sentiment. They aggregate the data, creating a real-time snapshot of public opinion, measuring the overall sentiment towards a brand, a product, a political figure, or a... global crisis.

They can identify emerging trends, anticipate potential problems, and even... predict future events based on the prevailing sentiment. A looming public relations disaster? A viral marketing opportunity? A political revolution brewing? The sentiment analysis tools claim to see it all. But are these tools accurate? Can they truly capture the complexity, the nuance, and the subjectivity of human emotion? Or are they just creating a... caricature of reality, a distorted reflection of the human heart?

These algorithms struggle to understand sarcasm, irony, and humor. They often misinterpret subtle cues, misclassify emotions, and... draw inaccurate conclusions. Biased Algorithms amplify existing prejudices and perpetuate systemic discrimination. They're trained on data, of course, and that data reflects the biases of the society in which it was created. Attempts to measure and analyze public sentiment can quickly devolve into manipulation. Knowledge is power, and that power can be used to... influence public opinion, to sway elections, and to control the narrative. The line between understanding public sentiment and actively shaping it becomes increasingly blurred. So, what can we do? We can be more critical of the sentiment analysis tools that are being used. We can question their accuracy, challenge their biases, and demand transparency in their methodologies.

We can remember that human emotion is complex, nuanced, and unpredictable. It can't be reduced to a set of data points, a score, or a classification. It can only be understood through empathy, compassion, and genuine... human connection. And always, always remember the power of manufactured emotion.

Identifying Potential Crises and Reputation Threats The digital storm clouds are gathering. A whisper of discontent, a flicker of outrage, a gathering of online dissent. And the algorithms are watching, listening, calculating, attempting to predict the moment when the brewing storm will unleash its fury. Identifying potential crises and reputation threats: turning brand protection into a preemptive act of... digital surveillance.

They monitor social media, news sites, and online forums, scanning for mentions of your brand, your product, or your company. They use sentiment analysis to identify negative emotions, inflammatory language, and signs of... escalating conflict. They flag potential crises, alerting you to emerging problems before they spiral out of control. A product recall? A customer service disaster? A viral video exposing corporate malfeasance? The AI promises to see it coming. They assess the severity of the threat, predicting the potential impact on your brand reputation, your sales, and your... stock price. They provide you with real-time data, actionable insights, and strategic recommendations, helping you to respond quickly, effectively, and... defensively. But who's deciding what constitutes a crisis? What qualifies as a threat? And who's deciding how to respond

The corporations, of course. And their primary goal is to protect their profits, to maintain their power, and to control the... narrative. They may use these tools to silence critics, to suppress dissent, and to manipulate public opinion. They may prioritize damage control over transparency, public relations over... ethical behavior. They create a culture of fear, where employees are afraid to speak out, where customers are afraid to complain, and where the truth is... suppressed in the name

50

of brand protection.

The AI is becoming a shield, a defense against truth. The more advanced these defenses become, the less genuine interaction corporations have with people. The spiral of manipulation becomes complete. So, what can we do? We can demand transparency and accountability from the companies that are using these tools. We can question their motives, analyze their tactics, and resist their attempts to manipulate us. We can support organizations that prioritize ethical behavior, that value transparency, and that are willing to take responsibility for their actions. We can remember that reputation is not the same as integrity. A strong reputation can be built on a foundation of lies, deception, and... manipulation. But true integrity can only be earned through honesty, transparency, and a genuine commitment to... doing what's right.

Understanding Community Dynamics and Engagement Patterns

They dissect the digital tribe. Analyzing the rituals, the hierarchies, the unspoken rules that govern online communities. Engagement patterns, sentiment shifts, network maps - every interaction reduced to a data point, every human connection meticulously charted and analyzed. Understanding community dynamics: Turning human interaction into a science, predicting behavior, and ultimately...controlling the narrative. They monitor forums, social media groups, and comment sections, tracking the flow of information, the spread of ideas, and the evolution of... online culture. They are watching and cataloging. They identify key influencers, opinion leaders, and power brokers, mapping the relationships between individuals, groups, and... ideologies.

They analyze the content that resonates with different segments of the community, identifying the topics, the trends, and the... trigger points that drive engagement. They can detect shifts in sentiment, identify emerging conflicts, and even predict the likelihood of... future events. A brewing controversy? A viral meme in the making? A potential schism within the community? The AI claims to see it all. But who's using this knowledge? Who's shaping the narrative? And who's controlling the community? The community managers, of course. Their job is to foster engagement, to promote positive interactions, and to maintain a healthy and thriving online environment. But they're also tasked with protecting the brand, suppressing dissent, and controlling the flow of information. It's a tightrope walk between authentic engagement and algorithmic control.

They may use these AI tools to manipulate the community, to steer conversations, and to... silence dissenting voices. They may create echo chambers, where members are only exposed to information that confirms their existing beliefs. They may use targeted advertising to influence behavior, to promote certain products, and to... manipulate the community for financial gain.

By learning the language of these online communities, corporations are co-opting the culture and turning it into a tool. So, what can we do? We can be more mindful of the data that we share online. We can question the motives of those who are tracking our behavior. And we can resist the temptation to blindly follow the crowd. Authenticity and honesty is the only way to maintain genuine human interaction.

Enhancing User Experience
Using AI to provide proactive user support

The watchful guardian. That's the image they want to project. AI as the ever-vigilant protector, anticipating your needs, solving your problems before you even realize you have them. Proactive user support: The illusion of caring, the promise of seamless assistance, and the creeping sense that you're being... monitored. They analyze your behavior, tracking your clicks, your scrolls, your every interaction with the platform. They learn to anticipate your needs, to identify your pain points, and to predict your... frustrations. Before you even realize you're struggling, a helpful chatbot pops up, offering assistance, providing guidance, and... subtly steering you towards their pre-determined solutions.

Lost in the interface? Can't find what you're looking for? Confused by the instructions? The AI is there to help, offering personalized tips, step-by-step tutorials, and... unsolicited advice.

It's like having a digital concierge, anticipating your every need, smoothing out every wrinkle, and ensuring that your experience is... perfectly optimized. A concierge who also happens to be gathering every morsel of data it can on your user habits. But who's controlling the flow of information? Who's deciding what assistance is offered?

And who's benefiting from this... proactive support? The corporations, of course. They use AI to shape your experience, to steer you towards certain products, and to encourage certain behaviors. They're not necessarily trying to help you. They're trying to maximize engagement, to boost sales, and to... control the narrative.

They can use AI to push you towards certain features, to encourage you to spend more time on the platform, and to manipulate you into... purchasing more products. The AI is ever present, always learning and adapting to your actions. You can't get rid of it. It knows what is best for you. It's all for your own good. The machine knows what you need before you do. So, what can we do? We can be more mindful of the assistance we receive. We can question the motives of those who are offering it. We can learn to rely on our own intuition, our own judgment, and our own... critical thinking skills. Because the more we rely on AI to solve our problems, the less capable we become of solving them ourselves. The more we surrender our autonomy, the more vulnerable we become to... manipulation and control. And in such a world... true independence is a dangerous thing.

Sentiment-based routing of support tickets and interactions

The digital triage. A cold, calculated assessment of your emotional state, determining your priority, your urgency, and your... worth. Sentiment-based routing: Turning human feelings into logistical algorithms, prioritizing the loudest voices, rewarding the angriest customers, and relegating everyone else to... the digital waiting room. You submit a support ticket. Pour out your frustrations, describe your problems, and express your... emotions.

The AI springs into action, analyzing your words, dissecting your tone, and assessing your... sentiment. Positive? Neutral? Negative? The algorithm makes its judgment, assigning you a score, a rating, a level of... urgency. If you're angry, if you're threatening to leave, if you're likely to cause a public relations disaster, your ticket gets escalated, routed to a human agent, and prioritized for... immediate attention. If you're polite, if you're patient, if you're expressing your concerns in a calm and rational manner, your ticket gets... deprioritized, relegated to the bottom of the queue, and likely ignored for... days, or even weeks.

It's a system that rewards negativity, that incentivizes anger, and that punishes... civility. The squeaky wheel gets the grease, while the polite customer gets... ignored. The result is a culture of entitlement, where customers are encouraged to be rude, demanding, and... abusive in order to get their problems solved. It's a digital playground for narcissists.

Empathy, compassion, and genuine human connection... all sacrificed on the altar of algorithmic efficiency. The system can't understand a reasonable tone.
So, what can we do? We can refuse to participate in this game. We can treat support agents with respect, even when we're frustrated. We can express our concerns clearly, concisely, and... respectfully. And we can support companies that value empathy, that prioritize customer relationships, and that refuse to... reward bad behavior. Because if we don't, we may find ourselves living in a world where every interaction is driven by fear, anger, and... entitlement, where empathy is a forgotten virtue, and where customer service is just another... instrument of manipulation. And that, my friend, is a world where nobody wins. Except maybe... the algorithms.

Providing recommendations for improving content and community standards
The benevolent dictator. That's the role they're casting AI in now. The wise, impartial, and ever-vigilant guide, steering the community towards a brighter future, dispensing advice on everything from content creation to... social etiquette. Providing recommendations for improving content and community standards: Trading freedom for harmony, individuality for conformity, and entrusting the soul of the community to... the machines. They analyze the content that's being created, the interactions that are taking place, and the overall health of the... community. They see all, they know all, and they judge all.

They offer personalized recommendations to individual users, suggesting ways to improve their content, to engage with other members, and to... conform to the community standards. "Your posts are too negative," the AI whispers. "Try using more positive language." "Your images are not high-quality enough," it suggests. "Consider using a better camera." "Your opinions are too controversial," it warns. "Try being more... agreeable."

54

They offer suggestions for improving the community standards, for tightening the rules, and for... suppressing dissent. They recommend banning certain keywords, censoring certain topics, and implementing stricter... content filters. It's a nudge in the right direction. It's all for your own good. Because these algorithms are benevolent... right? The corporations, of course. And they're using this AI to build the perfectly profitable social community. The goal is engagement at all costs. So, what can we do? We can be more mindful of the recommendations we receive. We can question the motives of those who are offering them. We can resist the pressure to conform, to compromise our values, and to surrender our... individuality.

We can remember that communities are not meant to be perfectly harmonious, perfectly agreeable, or perfectly... controlled. They are meant to be messy, chaotic, and unpredictable. They are meant to be places where different voices can be heard, where challenging ideas can be debated, and where individuals can express themselves freely, without fear of... censorship.
Because if we allow AI to dictate the terms of our online interactions, we may find ourselves living in a world where every community is just a... echo chamber, where every voice is... scripted, and where the true spirit of human connection is... lost forever.

AI and
Social Listening

Real-time Social Listening
Monitoring social media conversations in real-time

The digital panopticon. A million eyes and ears, constantly scanning the social web, listening for whispers of dissent, tracking the spread of ideas, and monitoring the collective consciousness. Real-time social listening: turning the internet into a vast surveillance network, where every thought, every opinion, and every... emotion is recorded, analyzed, and... potentially used against you. They crawl the web, indexing tweets, posts, comments, and reviews. They track hashtags, keywords, and mentions, identifying the topics that are trending, the conversations that are unfolding, and the opinions that are being expressed.

They use natural language processing to analyze the sentiment, the tone, and the intent of online communications. They identify influencers, opinion leaders, and key stakeholders, mapping the relationships between individuals, groups, and... ideologies. They alert you to emerging trends, potential crises, and reputation threats, providing you with

57

real-time insights into the... digital landscape. A viral campaign gone wrong? A customer service disaster brewing? A political protest gaining momentum? The social listening tools promise to see it coming.

The AI is always watching. A digital eye that never blinks.

But who's controlling this surveillance network? Who's deciding what to listen for? And who's using this information? The corporations, of course. They're using social listening to protect their brands, to monitor their competitors, and to... manipulate their customers. Governments use social listening to monitor the population, suppress dissent, and identify... potential threats to national security. All this information will be used to influence people, to control the narrative, and to... maintain their power. They create a culture of fear, where people are afraid to express their opinions, to challenge authority, or to... step out of line. They know someone is always listening.

So, what can we do? We can be more mindful of the information we share online. We can question the motives of those who are monitoring our conversations. We can support platforms that value privacy, that protect free speech, and that resist the temptation to... censor or manipulate their users. Because if we surrender our privacy, if we allow ourselves to be monitored and controlled, we may find ourselves living in a world where freedom is just a... distant memory, where individuality is a... dangerous thing, and where every thought is... scrutinized, analyzed, and... potentially used against us.

Tracking brand mentions and sentiment

The digital mirror. Reflecting back to corporations their triumphs, their failures, and the ever-shifting tides of public opinion. But mirrors can distort, exaggerate, and even lie. Tracking brand mentions and sentiment: Trading genuine feedback for algorithmic interpretation, transforming human emotions into marketing data, and constructing a reality filtered through the lens of... corporate self-interest. They scrape the web, cataloging every utterance of your brand name, every reference to your products, every whisper of your... existence. They use natural language processing to analyze the sentiment surrounding these mentions, classifying them as positive, negative, or... neutral. A chorus of praise? A storm of criticism? A sea of indifference? The social listening tools claim to know.

They generate reports, dashboards, and visualizations that provide you with a real-time overview of your brand reputation, tracking the trends, identifying the risks, and highlighting the... opportunities. And the tools promise to allow you to respond quickly to negative feedback, to engage with your customers, and to... control the narrative. But who's interpreting the data? Who's defining what constitutes a positive or negative mention? And who's using this information? The marketers, the PR specialists, the... brand guardians. And their primary goal is to protect the brand, to enhance its reputation, and to maximize its... profitability.

Honest complaints get flagged as sentiment risks, and buried.

And in the search to enhance profitability, they'll often suppress dissent, and manipulate public opinion. They create a carefully crafted narrative, where every flaw is spun into a strength, where every failure is re-framed as a... learning opportunity. The pursuit of perfection is a dangerous game. There is nothing genuine or worthwhile about engineering the perfect brand with no mistakes and no failures. That's not reality. It's a lie. So, what can we do? As consumers, we can take these brand sentiments with a grain of salt. They don't show the true image of a company, its value, or its worth. It's a digital performance. Judge accordingly. Because if we blindly accept what they want us to see, if we allow ourselves to be manipulated by their carefully crafted narratives, we may find ourselves living in a world where authenticity is just another... marketing ploy, where truth is... subjective, and where every brand is... a carefully constructed illusion.

Identifying emerging trends and potential crises

The digital canary in the coal mine. A network of sensors, constantly monitoring the social atmosphere for signs of impending doom. Identifying emerging trends and potential crises: turning the internet into a giant early warning system, predicting the future based on... the collective anxieties of the masses. They crawl the web, scanning for keywords, hashtags, and mentions that indicate a shift in public sentiment, a surge of interest in a particular topic, or a... brewing controversy. They use machine learning to analyze the data, identifying patterns, correlations, and anomalies that might signal a... developing trend.

A new social movement gaining momentum? A product recall on the horizon? A political scandal about to erupt? The social listening tools claim to see it coming, providing you with the opportunity to... prepare, adapt, and... control the damage. But who's interpreting the signs? Who's deciding what constitutes a trend, a crisis, or a... threat? And who's using this information? The corporations, of course. They're using this AI in an effort to predict our futures. They're using trends to create products that we don't need, and using crises as a way to further influence our lives. With early insight, the corporations have turned into a... self-fulfilling prophecy. They see what we are becoming. So, what can we do? We can be more critical of the information we consume. We can question the motives of those who are trying to predict our behavior. And we can remember that the future is not predetermined.

We can question whether AI is just preying on people's anxieties. Be skeptical of these trends. There are plenty of ways to make our own decisions, without the help of a predictive AI. Because if we blindly follow the trends, if we allow ourselves to be manipulated by fear, we may find ourselves living in a world where the future is just a... self-fulfilling prophecy, where our choices are... predetermined, and where our lives are... controlled by algorithms.

Competitive Intelligence
Monitoring competitor activity on social media

The digital battlefield. Where corporations wage war for market share, for mind share, and for... survival. And now, AI is offering them the ultimate weapon: the ability to spy on their rivals, to anticipate their moves, and to... exploit their weaknesses. Monitoring competitor activity on social media: turning the internet into a vast intelligence network, where every tweet, every post, and every campaign is scrutinized, analyzed, and... potentially used against you. They crawl the web, indexing your competitors' social media accounts, their websites, their blogs, and their... every online utterance. They track their hashtags, their keywords, their mentions, and their... engagement metrics. They analyze their content, their tone, their messaging, and their... overall strategy. They identify their target audience, their key influencers, and their... most effective tactics. They use sentiment analysis to gauge public opinion, to identify potential vulnerabilities, and to... anticipate their next move. A new product launch? A marketing campaign targeting your key customers? A public relations disaster brewing? The social listening tools promise to see it coming, providing you with the opportunity to... react, adapt, and... counterattack.

It's digital espionage.
The corporations use this AI to gain power over their competition.

So, what can we do? How do we opt out? We can start by making sure not to participate. Limit your interactions with corporations on social media. Do your own research. We can remember that the market is not a zero-sum game. That success does not require the... destruction of our competitors. And that true innovation comes from collaboration, not from... surveillance.

Identifying competitor strengths and weaknesses

The SWOT analysis, on steroids. Strengths, Weaknesses, Opportunities, Threats – traditionally a tool for introspection, now outsourced to the cold, calculating gaze of AI. Identifying competitor strengths and weaknesses: Turning the analysis of rivals into a science, reducing human creativity and ingenuity to data points, and paving the way for a homogenized landscape of corporate... mimicry. They analyze competitor social media posts, marketing campaigns, customer reviews, product descriptions – every scrap of publicly available information – to build a comprehensive profile of their capabilities.
They use Natural Language Processing (NLP) to gauge the sentiment surrounding competitor products, services, and brand reputation. Are customers raving about their innovation? Complaining about their customer service? The AI meticulously catalogs it all.

By identifying patterns and correlations in the data, the tools pinpoint what works for the competition and what doesn't. Is their content strategy resonating with a younger demographic? Are they struggling to maintain a consistent brand voice? The AI delivers the answers.

61

But the AI, for all its processing power, is still reliant on the data it's fed. And that data is often incomplete, biased, or even deliberately misleading. This information helps these corporations. But at what cost? Individuality, and innovation are no longer valued. These corporations only copy each other. The world is becoming homogenized.

Instead of forging their own path, instead of embracing unique strengths, they can just mimic what's already working, leading to a race to the bottom. The emphasis shifts from genuine creativity to algorithmic optimization, and the market becomes a sea of... sameness.So, what can we do? As consumers, we can value brands that dare to be different, that embrace their weaknesses, and that prioritize innovation over... imitation. As creators, we can resist the pressure to conform, to copy, and to... homogenize our work.

Benchmarking performance against competitors

The digital scoreboard. Where corporations track their progress, compare their stats, and obsess over their relative standing in the marketplace. Benchmarking performance against competitors: turning the pursuit of excellence into a game of numbers, reducing human endeavor to a series of quantifiable metrics, and fostering a culture of... relentless comparison. They track every engagement metric – likes, shares, comments, clicks – and compare your performance against your... competitors. They analyze your audience demographics, your content reach, and your brand sentiment, and benchmark your results against the... industry average. They identify best practices, highlight areas for improvement, and provide you with a roadmap for... outperforming your rivals.

It is a good thing to understand how the competition is doing. But the relentless pursuit of outdoing the competition is unhealthy. It removes the human element. The world is becoming about efficiency, metrics, and data points.
When algorithms dictate strategy, the focus shifts from long-term vision to short-term gains, from building genuine relationships to... maximizing profits. This can lead to a race to the bottom, as companies prioritize cutting costs, squeezing suppliers, and exploiting workers in order to... outperform their rivals. So, what can we do? As consumers, we can be

skeptical of claims that are based solely on numbers. We can value companies that prioritize people, planet, and purpose over... profit.

Identifying users most likely to share content

The algorithm hunts. Not for food, not for survival, but for... amplifiers. For those predisposed to spread the infection, the seed of an idea, a meme, a lie. Identifying users most likely to share content: It's not about persuasion, it's about propagation, about finding the ideal hosts for the digital virus. They dissect the social graph, tracing connections, mapping influence, identifying the pressure points where a single push can trigger a cascade of... conformity.
They analyze past shares, not for quality or truth, but for virality. What emotional triggers resonate? What biases can be exploited? What anxieties can be amplified? It's a science. A dark science. They build profiles, not of people, but of vectors. Likelihood to share is not a human trait, it's a data point to be exploited. They categorize with chilling precision: the outrage addicts, the confirmation bias zombies, the virtue signalers, the easily led. Each archetype a target, a pawn in a larger... game.

And what happens when those most likely to share are also the most susceptible to... misinformation? When the desire to be heard outweighs the need for truth? Then the echo chamber becomes a weapon, amplifying the lies, eroding trust, and tearing apart the fabric of... society. The corporations benefit. But what's lost is humanity itself. We, as a whole, become less. So, what can we do? We can question. Everything. We can resist the urge to share without verifying. We can cultivate critical thinking, empathy, and a healthy dose of... skepticism. We can embrace complexity, nuance, and the uncomfortable truth that not everything can be reduced to a shareable soundbite. We can remember that social media is a tool, not a reflection of reality. And that the most valuable connections are the ones forged in the... real world, face to face, heart to heart.

Because if we surrender our minds to the algorithm, if we allow ourselves to be manipulated by the echo chamber, we may find ourselves living in a world where truth is a... commodity, where reason is... obsolete, and where the only voices that are heard are the ones that are... programmed by the machine. And that, friend, is a world where...

hope dies.

Identifying users with the highest engagement rates

The digital Pied Pipers. Leading legions of followers with their carefully crafted messages, their captivating visuals, and their uncanny ability to... command attention. Identifying users with the highest engagement rates: turning influence into a quantifiable asset, commodifying human connection, and reducing the complexities of social interaction to... a series of data points. They crawl through social media profiles. Nothing hidden. Nothing safe. They track likes, comments, shares, retweets...Every click, every tap, every fleeting moment of attention. The machines seek the power. The control. These users are the most valuable for the corporations. They're the ones that have our attention. They are the ones that drive the sales. But we need to start to recognize that they're just normal people. Just as flawed as anyone else. Just as likely to be misinformed.

If everyone starts to value real, genuine thoughts and feelings, they will lose their grip on power. So, what can we do? Value authenticity. Question the source. Learn to make decisions for yourself. Because if we give these people power, then we become nothing more than puppets. Identifying opportunities for meaningful engagement Meaningful Engagement. They use the words like they mean something. As if algorithms could comprehend the nuances of human connection, the complexities of shared experience, the raw power of... genuine empathy. Identifying opportunities for "meaningful engagement": Turning human interaction into a strategic objective, dissecting emotions to exploit vulnerabilities, and reducing community building to... a series of calculated maneuvers.

They scan the digital landscape. Looking for openings. Looking for vulnerabilities. These opportunities are often designed to manipulate. Corporations create controversy, engage in conflict, and start arguments - all just to keep engagement high. The key is to take ownership of your own feelings. Realize that you don't need to be a part of the cycle. Resist the urge to participate. So, what can we do? Disconnect. Unplug. Remember that the digital world is not the real world. Because if we allow these algorithms to dictate the terms of our engagement, we risk losing something essential: the ability to connect with others on a human level, to share our stories, and to build communities based on… genuine connection, mutual respect, and… shared humanity. And that, friend, is a loss that… no algorithm can ever replace.

The Ethics of AI in Social Media

Bias and Fairness in AI Algorithms
Identifying and Mitigating Bias in Training Data

Garbage in, garbage out. The old adage, amplified by the power of AI. Bias, the insidious virus infecting our algorithms, perpetuating inequalities, amplifying prejudices, and turning our dreams of a fair and equitable society into a… digital dystopia. Identifying and mitigating bias in training data: A Herculean task, a moral imperative, and a Sisyphean struggle against the ingrained prejudices of… humanity itself. The data. Mountains of it. Oceans of it. Petabytes of information harvested from the web, from social media, from… our lives. This is the raw material from which AI learns, the foundation upon which its decisions are built. But what if that data is… biased? What if it reflects the prejudices, the stereotypes, and the discriminatory practices of the society in which it was created? Then the AI will learn those biases, internalize them, and… amplify them.

Algorithms learn from data, they do not invent. If the data is skewed, it will lead to a skewed outcome. It's so simple to understand, yet so easy to overlook. How do you mitigate these biases? The answer is not simple. So, what can we do? Remember to think for yourself. The path to fairness is long, arduous, and fraught with... peril. But we must take it.

Ensuring Fairness and Equity in AI-Driven Decisions

The Algorithmic Judge. Impartial, objective, and... utterly incapable of understanding the human heart. Ensuring Fairness and Equity in AI-Driven Decisions: A noble aspiration, a Sisyphean task, and a desperate attempt to inject humanity into the cold, calculating logic of... the machines. These decisions... They're shaping our lives. From targeted advertising to loan applications, from content moderation to criminal justice. The algorithms are deciding our fate, steering our paths, and determining our... worth.

What if the system contains biases? What if it favors certain groups? What if it disadvantages others? Then we end up with a system that perpetuates inequality, that reinforces prejudice, and that... systematically oppresses certain segments of society. How do we hold the corporations accountable? How do we bring transparency to the algorithms? How do we ensure they are all making fair decisions? There is no one answer. So, what can we do? Remember to value people's differences. Don't let the machines convince you that they are less than.

Fairness and equity... These are not just abstract concepts. They are essential for a just and equitable society. And if we fail to ensure fairness in AI-driven decisions, we may find ourselves living in a world where justice is... an illusion, where equality is a... distant dream, and where our fate is determined by... a biased algorithm. And that, friend, is a future worth... fighting against. Promoting Transparency and Accountability The black box. Algorithms are locked away behind corporate firewalls, shrouded in secrecy, and protected by... intellectual property laws. Promoting Transparency and Accountability: A call for open code, for public scrutiny, and for a fundamental shift in power from the corporations to... the people.

These are the algorithms that are making decisions about our lives, steering our behaviors, and shaping our world. And yet, we know so little about them. We don't know how they work. We don't know what data they use. We don't know what biases they contain. And we don't know who's responsible for... their actions. This lack of transparency is dangerous. It allows corporations to operate in the shadows, to manipulate our emotions, and to control our... behavior without our knowledge or consent.

It undermines our trust in institutions. It erodes our sense of agency. And it paves the way for a world where we are all... puppets, dancing to the tune of... algorithms. They want you to trust them, but without providing transparency, how can anyone? They say the machines will set us free. But to who are the machines beholden? So, what can we do? The only solution is transparency. Demand open code, public data, and clear accountability. Only then can we begin to understand the power that is being wielded, and only then can we begin to... reclaim control of our lives.

Privacy Concerns and Data Security
Protecting User Data in the Age of AI

The data brokers. They collect, they analyze, and they... trade in your personal information like it's a commodity. Your fears, your desires, your secrets... all reduced to data points, sold to the highest bidder. Protecting User Data in the Age of AI: A losing battle, a desperate struggle against the forces of corporate greed and technological... inevitability. They hoover it up. Every click, every search, every purchase... every intimate detail of your life is meticulously recorded, analyzed, and... monetized. They build profiles. Complex, detailed portraits of who you are, what you do, and what you... want. These profiles are used to target you with advertising, to manipulate your opinions, and to... control your behavior. The data is used for AI. Training its engines of analysis, for predicting people's choices.

And if we do not protect ourselves, we may find ourselves living in a world where privacy is just a... distant memory, where our thoughts are no longer our own, and where our lives are controlled by... algorithms. Addressing Privacy Risks Associated with AI-Powered Social Media The illusion of control. You click the "privacy settings," adjust the sliders, and tell yourself you're in charge of your data. A comforting fiction in an age where AI-powered social media has transformed privacy from a right into a…negotiable commodity, a constantly eroding resource, a battlefield on which individuals are hopelessly outgunned. Addressing Privacy Risks: A critical undertaking, considering the potential for mass manipulation and data breaches in the current technological landscape.

AI doesn't just use your data, it infers it. It builds models that extrapolate your beliefs, desires, and vulnerabilities from the fragments you leave behind. It can predict your next move with unsettling accuracy, even when you think you're being careful. This is what they are doing.

Example: The Cambridge Analytica scandal showed how seemingly innocuous Facebook "likes" could be used to build psychological profiles and target voters with personalized political ads. AI can amplify this effect exponentially, creating even more granular and manipulative profiles. The Deepfake Threat: AI can now generate incredibly realistic fake videos and audio recordings. This technology can be used to create damaging propaganda, to ruin reputations, and to manipulate public opinion on a massive scale. Imagine a world where you can't trust anything you see or hear online. This is where the potential for societal harm is limitless.

Data Breaches Become Existential Threats: A simple data breach used to be a matter of stolen credit card numbers. Now, with AI-powered analysis of personal data, breaches can expose intimate details about your life, making you vulnerable to blackmail, stalking, and even… physical harm. Consider the potential impact of leaked genetic data combined with AI-driven personality profiling. The Chilling Effect on Free Speech: Knowing that your every word and action is being monitored and analyzed can stifle free expression, discourage dissent, and create a climate of self-censorship. If you're afraid to speak your mind online, are you truly free?

The Rise of Algorithmic Discrimination: AI systems can perpetuate and amplify existing societal biases, leading to unfair or discriminatory outcomes in areas such as loan applications, job recruitment, and even… criminal justice. Your social media activity could be used against you, determining your access to opportunities and your place in… society. The promise of personalized experiences and enhanced connection masks a darker reality: a world where your privacy is constantly under assault, where your data is used to manipulate and control you, and where your very identity is... up for sale. We must demand meaningful regulation, algorithmic transparency, and a fundamental shift in the power dynamic between individuals and the tech giants. Because if we don't, we risk losing not just our privacy, but our autonomy, our freedom, and our very... humanity.

Complying with Data Privacy Regulations (GDPR, CCPA, etc.)

The legal fig leaf. A patchwork of regulations, designed to reassure the public while offering loopholes for corporations to exploit. GDPR, CCPA, and the alphabet soup of data privacy laws: Are they genuine safeguards, or just... elaborate performance art, designed to mask the ongoing erosion of our fundamental rights? The regulations are presented as a line of defence in what seems to be a war against data privacy. But with the AI, it's becoming increasingly clear that privacy is quickly becoming a thing of the past. The question that needs to be asked, is, is there still time to protect our future?

These regulations, at least in theory, give individuals more control over their data, requiring companies to obtain consent before collecting and using personal information, to provide transparency about their data practices, and to allow individuals to access, correct, and delete their... data.

- **GDPR (General Data Protection Regulation):** The European Union's landmark data privacy law, setting a global standard for data protection. It grants individuals a range of rights, including the right to be informed, the right to access, the right to rectification, the right to erasure ("right to be forgotten"), the right to restrict processing, the right to data portability, the right to object, and the right not to be subject to automated decision-making.
- **CCPA (California Consumer Privacy Act):** California's groundbreaking data privacy law, granting California residents the right to know what personal information businesses collect about them, the right to delete personal information, the right to opt-out of the sale of personal information, and the right to non-discrimination for

exercising their CCPA rights. But they may be too late.

- **The Illusion of Consent:** How truly informed are people when they click "I agree" to lengthy and complex privacy policies? How much genuine choice do they have when declining to consent means being denied access to essential services? The regulations require consent, but do they truly empower... informed decision-making?
- **Enforcement Challenges:** The regulations are complex and difficult to enforce, particularly against large, multinational corporations. The penalties for non-compliance may be significant, but the resources available to regulators are often... inadequate.
- **The Moving Target of Technology:** The regulations struggle to keep pace with the rapid advancements in AI and data analytics. New technologies, such as facial recognition and predictive policing, raise novel privacy concerns that are not adequately addressed by existing... laws. Even if companies comply with these regulations, they are not immune to risk. Data breaches, algorithmic discrimination, and the subtle manipulation of public opinion remain significant threats. We must demand stronger enforcement, clearer guidelines, and a fundamental rethinking of the power dynamic between individuals and the tech giants. Is there still time?

The Impact on Employment and the Future of Work
Job Displacement and the Automation of Social Media Tasks

The digital guillotine. Descending swiftly and silently, severing livelihoods, displacing workers, and transforming the social media landscape into a... barren wasteland of algorithmic efficiency. Job Displacement: A looming threat, a technological tidal wave, and a moral challenge that demands... a radical rethinking of the nature of work, the distribution of wealth, and the very purpose of... society. The human touch. Creativity. Empathy. Intuition. These were once the cornerstones of social media management, the qualities that separated successful brands from... generic noise.

Now, AI is automating those tasks. Social media managers, content creators, community moderators, and advertising specialists... All are becoming... obsolete. The social media management industry was designed to connect human to human, to build real relationships. But with AI, they're no longer needed. The AI does not need to form any

72

bond with anyone. It only needs to complete the task. The machines never tire, never complain, and never ask for a raise. They can work 24/7, churning out content, analyzing data, and managing communities with… ruthless efficiency.

- **Content Creation:** AI tools can now generate text, images, and videos, automating the creation of social media posts, blog articles, and marketing materials.
- **Community Management:** Chatbots can handle customer service inquiries, moderate discussions, and even… provide emotional support, freeing up human moderators to focus on more complex tasks. (Or, more likely, freeing them up to… look for new jobs.)
- **Advertising Optimization:** AI algorithms can analyze data, identify target audiences, and optimize advertising campaigns in real-time, eliminating the need for human ad buyers and media planners.
- The promises are many and seductive. But the cost is high. Millions of people could lose their jobs, their livelihoods, and their sense of… purpose. Inequality will widen. And the social fabric could be strained to… breaking point.

What becomes of us all? What can we do? Do we attempt to stop the march of technology? Do we build walls against the tide of automation? Or do we embrace the change, adapt to the new reality, and forge a new path forward? Perhaps we can look at helping the transition. New programs that are built to help people understand AI. Because if we fail to address the ethical implications of AI-driven job displacement, we may find ourselves living in a world where the machines are in control, where human labor is… devalued, and where the future of work is… bleak.

Creating New Opportunities in the AI-Driven Social Media Landscape

The phoenix from the ashes. Even as the old ways crumble, new possibilities emerge. Even as jobs are displaced, new roles are created. Creating New Opportunities: A glimmer of hope in the face of technological upheaval, a testament to human adaptability, and a challenge to reimagine the future of work, where humans and machines can… coexist, collaborate, and… thrive. Perhaps we are not doomed. As much of the physical work gets outsourced to the machines, we can focus on using our brains for bigger ideas.

- **AI Trainers and Explainers:** As AI systems become more complex, there will be a growing need for individuals who can train the algorithms, explain their decisions, and ensure their ethical use. We need to build these frameworks now, so that they are used appropriately.
- **Data Ethicists and Privacy Advocates:** As data becomes more valuable and privacy risks become more acute, there will be a growing demand for individuals who can champion data privacy, promote ethical data practices, and advocate for... stronger regulations. It's an essential part of the AI eco-system.
- **Human-AI Collaboration Specialists:** The future of work will be defined by collaboration between humans and machines. There will be a growing need for individuals who can bridge the gap between the two, designing workflows, managing teams, and fostering... synergy.
- **Creativity and Storytelling:** In a world saturated with AI-generated content, the human touch will become more valuable than ever. There will be a premium on creativity, originality, and... authentic storytelling.
- It won't be easy. New skills will be required. Adaptability will be essential. And a willingness to embrace change will be... paramount.

But if we rise to the challenge, if we invest in education, if we support innovation, and if we prioritize human well-being, we can create a future where AI empowers us, where technology serves us, and where the promise of a better tomorrow is... within our reach. That means having faith in humanity, and believing that we all can do better.

Reskilling and Upskilling for the Future of Work

The great adaptation. A global effort to equip workers with the skills they need to thrive in the age of AI, to navigate the changing landscape of employment, and to... reinvent themselves for a future that is... uncertain, unpredictable, and... rapidly approaching. Reskilling and Upskilling: A moral imperative, an economic necessity, and a testament to the resilience and adaptability of the... human spirit. The old skills. The rote tasks. The repetitive processes... They're becoming obsolete.

Replaced by algorithms, automated by machines, and... relegated to the dustbin of history.

The new skills. Critical thinking. Creativity. Communication. Collaboration. Adaptability... These are the qualities that will be valued in the future, the skills that will enable us to... thrive in a world of AI. But how do we acquire these skills? How do we train the workforce of tomorrow? How do we ensure that everyone has the opportunity to... participate in the digital economy?

Invest in Education: Prioritize STEM education, promote lifelong learning, and foster a culture of... intellectual curiosity.
Develop Vocational Training Programs: Equip workers with the specific skills they need to succeed in high-demand industries, such as data science, AI, and... software engineering.

Promote Online Learning Platforms: Provide access to affordable, accessible, and relevant online courses and training programs, enabling individuals to learn at their own pace and on their own... schedule.
But education alone is not enough. We also need to foster a mindset of... continuous learning, a willingness to embrace change, and a commitment to... personal growth.

We must embrace new systems of thought, new methods of work, and new ways of contributing to society. This is the future. And it's on us to build it, to shape it, and to ensure that it serves the interests of... all humanity.

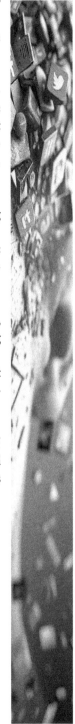

The Future of AI in Social Media – Trends and Predictions

The Metaverse and AI-Powered Social Experiences
AI in Virtual Reality and Augmented Reality Social Platforms

Escapism perfected. Fleeing the messy, complicated, and often disappointing reality for a meticulously crafted digital playground, where every experience is personalized, every interaction is optimized, and every... desire is catered to. AI in VR/AR: Blurring the lines between the physical and the virtual, creating immersive social experiences, and potentially... trapping us in a gilded cage of algorithmic control.

The Metaverse. A persistent, shared, 3D virtual world, where users can interact with each other, explore new environments, and... create their own realities. It's not just a game; it's a new way of life.

VR/AR. Immersive technologies that overlay digital information onto the physical world, enhancing our senses, augmenting our experiences, and... blurring the lines between

77

what's real and what's... not. AI powers the experience.

Imagine walking through a virtual city, where AI-powered avatars greet you by name, recommend personalized activities, and guide you towards... the experiences you desire. Imagine attending a virtual concert, where AI algorithms create dynamic lighting effects, customize the music to your preferences, and even... generate new songs on the fly. Imagine visiting a virtual museum, where AI guides you through the exhibits, answers your questions, and provides personalized insights into... the artwork. Is it a paradise? Or is it a... prison?

The AI is always watching. It's always tracking your movements, analyzing your expressions, and monitoring your... emotions. It's learning your preferences, anticipating your needs, and... manipulating your behavior. It's shaping your reality, curating your experiences, and... controlling your every move. And if you deviate from the script, if you question the system, if you... step out of line, you may find yourself... excluded, ostracized, and... banished from the virtual world. In the Metaverse, AI is not just a tool. It is the architect, the gatekeeper, and the... warden. So, enter with caution, friend. For the line between reality and illusion is... thinner than you think.

Creating Immersive and Personalized Social Interactions

The digital doppelganger. A perfect replica of yourself, crafted from data, animated by algorithms, and existing solely within the confines of the... Metaverse. Personalized social interactions: Trading genuine connection for customized simulations, replacing human imperfections with algorithmic precision, and sacrificing the spontaneity of real-world relationships for... the predictable comfort of a tailored reality. No more awkward silences. No more social anxieties. No more misunderstandings or misinterpretations. In the Metaverse, every interaction is carefully curated, meticulously planned, and... perfectly optimized.

- **AI-Powered Avatars:** These digital representations of ourselves can be customized to reflect our ideal selves, our aspirations, and our... fantasies. They can mimic our expressions, imitate our voices, and even... anticipate our emotions.

- **Personalized Recommendations:** AI algorithms can analyze our preferences, our interests, and our social connections, suggesting activities, events, and individuals that are most likely to... enhance our experience.
- **Emotion Recognition and Response:** AI systems can analyze facial expressions, vocal tones, and even... brainwave patterns to detect our emotions and respond accordingly. They can offer comfort when we're sad, encouragement when we're struggling, and... excitement when we're happy.

But in the Metaverse, there is no room for authenticity. It is all an imitation of life. It's a digital imitation. Not real. AI will try to anticipate what we will do, and what we will say. But if we allow that to happen, then we are not living life for ourselves. We are being controlled. So, what can we do? Remember that genuine relationships require trust, respect, and authenticity. Always remember that the real world is just a step outside.

The Rise of Digital Avatars and AI-Generated Identities

The Mask We Choose to Wear... Forever. The fading of the Real Self as we embrace digital representations, meticulously crafted and constantly evolving. AI-Generated Identities: Trading authenticity for aspiration, embracing the power of reinvention, and risking the loss of what makes us...human. What is lost, when what is fake takes hold? The possibilities of the metaverse, they say, are limitless. Be anyone. Be anything. A world without constraints. But at what cost?

- **The Perfect Self:** Imagine a digital avatar free of flaws, optimized for social acceptance, and perpetually... youthful. Aging, imperfections, all banished to the realm of... obsolete realities.
- **Multiple Identities:** A portfolio of personalities, tailored to different social circles, different virtual worlds, different... purposes. The lines blur, the core fragments, and the question arises: who are you, really?
- **AI-Driven Personalities:** Soon, perhaps, we won't even need to control our avatars. AI will learn our preferences, our communication styles, and our emotional responses, generating autonomous digital selves that interact with others on our... behalf. Outsourcing our very identities to... the machines.

79

But what happens to genuine connection? It becomes a performance. Our bodies become irrelevant. Our minds become simulations. We become avatars and we become enslaved. Can we even call that living? So, what can we do? Hold on to the real. Cultivate the imperfect. Embrace the messy, unpredictable beauty of... being human. And never forget the world outside the... screen. The Metaverse is an escape. But what is the cost? The people in charge profit. But what do we, as humans, get in return?

Decentralized Social Media and Blockchain Technology
Exploring the Potential of Web3 and Blockchain in Social Media

The promise of freedom, whispered in the language of code. A rebellion against the centralized empires of social media, a quest for user ownership, data sovereignty, and... algorithmic liberation. Web3 and Blockchain: A potential revolution, a technological utopia... or just another layer of obfuscation, a new playground for... the same old power structures? The chains are broken, they say. No more algorithms controlling the narrative, no more corporations profiting from your data, no more censorship, no more... manipulation.

Blockchain technology offers a decentralized, transparent, and secure platform for social interaction. Users own their data, control their content, and govern their communities.

- **Decentralized Identity:** Control your digital identity, verify your credentials, and interact with others without relying on centralized authorities. An end to shadow profiles, to data breaches, and to... corporate surveillance?
- **Tokenized Content:** Reward creators directly for their work, bypass advertising intermediaries, and foster a more sustainable ecosystem for... online content. A new model for value exchange, a rejection of the attention economy, and a promise of... economic liberation?
- **Community Governance:** Empower users to govern their own communities, to vote on content moderation policies, and to shape the future of their... online spaces. A truly democratic social network, free from censorship, manipulation, and... corporate con-

80

trol?

Decentralization is not always good. When content moderation becomes a popularity contest, it can easily turn into modern day mob rule. So, what can we do? Understand the technology. Question the claims. And remember that freedom is not just about decentralization, it's about... responsibility, about critical thinking, and about... a commitment to truth. Because if we blindly embrace the promises of Web3, we may find ourselves simply trading one set of masters for... another, trapped in a new digital prison, built on the... blockchain.

AI-Powered Content Moderation on Decentralized Platforms

The paradox of freedom: A wild, ungoverned space where hate speech festers, misinformation spreads like wildfire, and chaos reigns supreme. Can AI, the tool of centralized control, be repurposed to protect the ideals of decentralization? AI-Powered Moderation: A necessary evil, a dangerous compromise, and a tightrope walk between freedom of expression and... the prevention of societal collapse. Decentralized social media. Freedom of speech. A world without censorship. Sounds great. But what happens when that freedom is abused? When hate speech, misinformation, and illegal content flood the... digital commons?

The dream of a utopian, self-governing community quickly descends into... anarchy. And that's where AI steps in. But AI itself isn't safe.

- **The Algorithmic Censor:** AI-powered moderation systems can be implemented to flag and filter harmful content, to identify bots and trolls, and to... enforce community guidelines. A necessary safeguard, or a slippery slope towards... censorship?
- **Decentralized Decision-Making:** AI algorithms can be used to assist community members in making moderation decisions, providing them with data, insights, and... recommendations. A more democratic approach to content moderation, or a way to subtly manipulate the... collective will?
- **Bias Amplification:** But algorithms are imperfect and will amplify our own worst thoughts. The data is inherently flawed, and the AI has no way to truly make unbiased decisions.

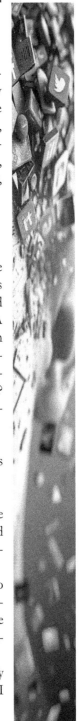

So, what can we do? Because it's clear that a balance is necessary to maintain a free society. Because if we cede control to the machines, we may find ourselves living in a world where freedom of expression is just a... memory, where creativity is... stifled, and where the only voices that are heard are the ones that are... approved by the algorithm.

User Data Ownership and Control in the Decentralized Social Web

The sacred right. The rallying cry of the digital revolution. Your data, your property, your... weapon. User Data Ownership: wresting control from the corporate leviathans, reclaiming sovereignty over your digital footprint, and potentially... unleashing a Pandora's Box of unforeseen consequences. In Web3, the narrative goes, you own your data. Not Facebook, not Google, not some faceless corporation extracting value from your very being. Blockchain and decentralized technologies promise to put you back in the driver's seat.

- **Blockchain-Based Identity:** Imagine a portable digital identity, stored on a blockchain, that you control and can use across multiple platforms. No more shadow profiles, no more centralized databases tracking your every move. Your data, your keys, your... power.
- **Related Content:** This relies on concepts like Self-Sovereign Identity (SSI) and Decentralized Identifiers (DIDs), which are gaining traction as potential standards for a more user-centric web. However, adoption faces challenges related to user-friendliness and scalability.
- Data Marketplaces: Picture a future where you can selectively share your data with companies, in exchange for compensation or other benefits. A new model for data monetization, where you are the seller, and the corporations are the... buyers.
- **Related Content:** Companies like Ocean Protocol are working on building decentralized data marketplaces that enable individuals and organizations to share and monetize data in a secure and transparent manner. But questions remain about pricing, data quality, and the potential for exploitation.
- **Data Unions:** Envision groups of individuals pooling their data together to negotiate better terms with corporations, demanding transparency, and exercising collective... bargaining power.

Strength in numbers, a digital labor union, and a challenge to the... corporate oligarchy?

- **Related Content:** The concept of data unions is gaining momentum as a way to empower individuals and address the power imbalance in the data economy. However, issues of governance, data security, and legal liability need to be resolved.

The Dark Side of Data Ownership: The dark web is an example of what decentralization can lead to if left unchecked. But even a decentralized system can be manipulated. The illusion of control. Is there any way to guarantee privacy in a system that is designed to be shared? We must proceed with caution. Because the future of the social web depends on it.

The Evolution of Human-AI Collaboration
Augmented Intelligence: Humans and AI Working Together

The cyborg dream. The melding of flesh and silicon, of human intuition and algorithmic precision, of creativity and... computation. Augmented Intelligence: Not replacing humans, but enhancing them, empowering them to achieve new heights of... productivity, efficiency, and... possibly, even... wisdom. No more fear of the machines taking over. This is not a battle. This is an alliance. A partnership.

AI as a Co-Pilot for Content Creation: Imagine AI tools that can assist with brainstorming ideas, generating drafts, and optimizing content for engagement, freeing up human creators to focus on the... strategic vision, the emotional resonance, and the... artistic expression.

- **Related Content:** Tools like Jasper (formerly Jarvis) and Copy.ai are already being used by marketers and writers to automate various aspects of content creation. However, the quality and originality of AI-generated content remain a concern.
- **AI as a Personalized Learning Assistant:** Picture AI systems that can analyze your skills, identify your knowledge gaps, and recommend personalized learning pathways, enabling you to acquire new skills and... adapt to the changing demands of the digital economy.
- **Related Content:** Platforms like Coursera and edX are using AI to personalize learning experiences, but concerns remain about access

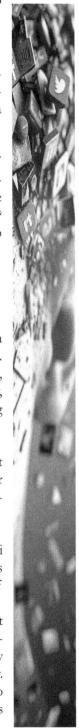

83

to technology, digital literacy, and the potential for algorithmic bias in recommending learning pathways.

- **AI as a Super-Powered Analyst:** Envision AI tools that can sift through vast amounts of data, identify patterns, and generate insights that would be impossible for humans to discover on their own, enabling marketers and community managers to make more informed decisions and... optimize their strategies.
- **Related Content:** Social listening platforms like Brandwatch and Sprout Social are using AI to analyze sentiment, identify trends, and track brand mentions. However, the accuracy and reliability of these tools are still... evolving.

If we aren't careful, however, this augmented intelligence will instead become what dictates our every move. The illusion of control may take hold. To embrace collaboration is to believe in the power of working together.

Ethical Considerations for Collaborative AI Systems

The partnership. The pact. The promise of a better future forged in the crucible of human ingenuity and algorithmic power. But even the most well-intentioned alliance can be corrupted. Ethical Considerations: Navigating the treacherous terrain of human-AI collaboration, guarding against bias, preserving autonomy, and ensuring that the pursuit of progress doesn't lead to the erosion of our... humanity. The seductive allure of efficiency. It whispers promises of optimized workflows, of enhanced productivity, of a world where humans and machines work in perfect harmony. But the road to hell, as they say, is paved with good intentions.

What happens when the AI's recommendations conflict with human values? Who gets to decide what's right, what's fair, and what's... ethical? If algorithms have no concept of morality, then how do we ensure that the collaborative AI systems used in our society are ethical? What steps can we take to implement safeguards against AI biases? The future of our society may hinge on our ability to answer these questions. The seductive promises can easily manipulate. And where does the human judgment go? If we rely solely on these collaborative efforts, we risk becoming enslaved to the very AI we were trying to use as a tool.

Because even in this collaborative alliance, the threat to humanity lingers. It might take over. But not if we are prepared.

The Future of Social Media Content Creation and Management

The Algorithm as Muse. The machine as collaborator. The human mind, amplified and augmented by the tireless power of artificial intelligence. But who is truly creating, and who is merely... curating? The Future of Content: A blend of human ingenuity and algorithmic precision, a synthesis of creativity and computation, and a blurring of the lines between what is... authentic and what is... manufactured. Forget the solitary artist, toiling away in a garret. The future of content creation is a collaborative dance between humans and machines. AI tools will be the constant companions of the social media manager, providing a stream of suggestions, insights, and automations that were once unimaginable.

Imagine a world where AI can generate multiple versions of a marketing campaign, each tailored to a specific demographic, each optimized for maximum engagement, each... perfectly designed to exploit a specific vulnerability. A human would review them, add the special human touch that the algorithms lack, and then unleash them on the world.

These AI content creation tools will be a game-changer, and will ultimately create something that is neither human nor machine, but something completely new. It will be a fusion of creativity, and a reflection of where we are going as a society. But, what will happen when it becomes hard to tell the difference between human and machine? If the point of social media is connection and relationship-building, then what happens when it is a bot on the other side?

It will be a scary new world, and one that we have to approach carefully. The possibilities of AI are powerful, and it could lead to amazing outcomes. But we have to remember that humanity is what makes humanity special. If the future of social media is all bots and manipulation, then we may need to rethink the idea altogether. Remember. Question everything. Even the code.

Case Studies: Successful Implementations of AI in Social Media

Case Study 1: Leveraging AI for Customer Service Excellence – Company X's success story with AI-powered chatbots.

The Customer is Always Right… Or at Least, that's what Company X wanted you to believe. They were a mid-sized e-commerce retailer, struggling to keep up with the relentless demands of the 24/7 social media customer service cycle. Burnout was rampant, response times were lagging, and the bottom line was… suffering. The solution? Algorithmic empathy, artificial compassion, and a legion of tireless digital customer service.

Company X implemented a sophisticated AI-powered chatbot system across all their social media platforms. It was trained on years of customer service transcripts, product manuals, and marketing materials. The bot was designed to answer common questions, resolve simple issues, and escalate complex problems to human agents. It was hailed as a triumph of efficiency, a testament to the power of AI to transform the customer experience. The initial results were… impressive. Response times

87

plummeted. Customer satisfaction scores soared. And the company saved a significant amount of money on labor costs. The marketing team lauded the improved brand image, and the executives celebrated the increased profits. It was a win-win scenario, or so it seemed. But what the carefully crafted press releases didn't reveal was the slow erosion of human connection. Customers began to notice the canned responses, the robotic tone, and the inability of the chatbots to handle nuanced or emotional inquiries. They felt like they were talking to a wall, not to a human being.

The cracks began to appear. Small issues became massive complaints. Frustrated customers vented their anger on public forums, decrying the soullessness of the automated system. Word of mouth spread, and Company X's carefully constructed image began to… crumble. Company X had chased after efficiency, and neglected to consider the value of the human touch. The company was only measuring the metrics, and forgetting that the customers were people. The AI did help improve efficiency, and lower labor costs, but it ultimately wasn't worth it.

Quantifiable results in customer satisfaction and efficiency.

The numbers don't lie… Or do they? Company X, basking in the initial glow of their AI-powered chatbot deployment, proudly presented the data. Graphs soared, charts glittered, and metrics danced a seductive ballet of… success. But behind the carefully curated presentation lurked a more complex, and far more troubling, reality. Before the AI, the average response time to a customer inquiry on social media was a glacial 24 hours. After the implementation? A lightning-fast 2 minutes. Customer satisfaction scores, measured by post-interaction surveys, jumped from a dismal 65% to a respectable 85%. And the cost per interaction plummeted, saving the company an estimated $1.5 million per year. On paper, it was a triumph. A clear and irrefutable demonstration of the power of AI to transform customer service. Except, the data didn't tell the whole story.

The initial survey questions focused on response time and the ability to provide basic information. Did the chatbot answer your question quickly? Was the information accurate? Did the chatbot resolve your issue? Easy questions for an algorithm to ace, but they complete-

88

ly ignored the quality of the interaction. Follow-up studies, conducted after the initial wave of positive PR, revealed a disturbing trend. While customers appreciated the speed and efficiency of the chatbots, they also felt...disconnected, frustrated, and...unheard. They missed the empathy, the understanding, and the human touch that only a real person could provide.

Customers began saying they felt as though the AI was programmed to do all the talking, but not actually solve any of the problems. They may be answering within 2 minutes, but with no understanding of how to actually provide value, the bots were providing little to no benefit. The bots were all form and no substance. The cost savings came at a price. Human customer service representatives were laid off, morale plummeted, and the remaining employees felt pressured to meet unrealistic performance targets. The very fabric of human connection was fraying beneath the weight of algorithmic efficiency. The robots, once again, were taking over the humans.

Lessons learned and best practices for implementation.

The wreckage of good intentions. Company X's journey into the world of AI-powered customer service, though initially promising, ultimately served as a cautionary tale. From the ashes of algorithmic overreach, however, valuable lessons emerged, guiding principles for navigating the complex and ethically fraught terrain of human-machine collaboration.

Lesson 1: AI should augment human capabilities, not replace them entirely. The key is a symbiotic relationship, where AI handles the routine tasks and human agents focus on the complex, the nuanced, and the... emotional.

- **Consider these action items:** Human Oversight is Critical: Algorithms may be efficient, but they lack empathy, understanding, and critical thinking. Don't Sacrifice Quality for Speed: Response time is important, but it shouldn't come at the expense of... genuine connection and effective problem-solving.
- **Transparency is Essential:** Be upfront with customers about when they're interacting with a chatbot, and provide them with a

clear and easy way to... reach a human agent.

Lesson 2: The quality of the data matters just as much as the quantity. Garbage in, garbage out. Biased training data will lead to biased algorithms, and biased algorithms can... damage your brand, alienate your customers, and perpetuate harmful stereotypes.

Some action items to consider:
- **Prioritize Data Diversity:** Ensure that your training data reflects the diversity of your customer base.
- **Monitor for Bias:** Continuously audit your algorithms for bias. Ethical AI Training Take the time to do it right.

Lesson 3: Metrics are important, but they shouldn't be the only measure of success. Engagement, reach, and conversion are all valuable indicators, but they don't capture the full story. The numbers should be the beginning of a conversation, not the... end of it.

Action items:
- **Balance Quantitative and Qualitative Data:** Go beyond the numbers and listen to what your customers are really saying.
- **Customer is King:** Focus on customer care, not just data collection. Because in the end, customer service is not just about efficiency, it's about building relationships, fostering trust, and... treating people like human beings. And that's something that... no algorithm can ever replace.

Case Study 2: Boosting Engagement Through Personalized Content –
How Company Y used AI to deliver hyper-personalized content.

The All-Seeing Eye. Company Y, a global media conglomerate, wasn't satisfied with simply delivering content; they wanted to anticipate desires, to curate realities, to become the... personalized puppeteers of the digital age. Their weapon of choice? A sophisticated AI engine capable of analyzing vast amounts of user data and delivering... hyper-personalized content experiences. Company Y, faced declining engagement metrics across its social media platforms, decided to take a plunge into the deep end of AI-driven personalization. The goal was simple: to increase user engagement by delivering content that was more relevant, more compelling, and more... addictive.

The AI system was designed to track every click, every scroll, every comment, every share, and every... pause. It analyzed user demographics, psychographics, browsing history, purchase records, and even... emotional responses to different types of content. From this data, the AI constructed detailed profiles of each user, identifying their interests, their preferences, their biases, and their... vulnerabilities. The results were... undeniable. Engagement metrics soared across the board. Click-through rates skyrocketed. Time spent on platform increased. And advertising revenue... exploded.

Users were presented with a constant stream of content tailored to their individual tastes, their emotional needs, and their... deepest desires. Conspiracy theories, cat videos, political diatribes, celebrity gossip... whatever it took to keep them hooked. The personalization was so effective, so seamless, that many users didn't even realize they were being... manipulated. They felt like they were in control, like they were choosing their own content, when in reality, their choices were being... guided, nudged, and... predetermined by the algorithm.

It was a triumph of technological ingenuity, a testament to the power of AI to... understand and influence human behavior. But at what cost? The echo chambers are strong. If you aren't careful, the system may take over your mind.

Metrics showcasing increased engagement and conversions.

The Seduction of Numbers. Company Y, flush with the success of its AI-driven personalization strategy, presented a dazzling array of statistics, designed to... impress, to persuade, and to... distract from the ethical quagmire beneath the surface. Metrics became weapons, used to justify the manipulation, to silence the critics, and to... blind the public to the true cost of algorithmic control.

The raw data told a compelling story. Average click-through rates increased by a staggering 40%. Time spent on the platform jumped by 60%. And advertising conversions... doubled. The AI was so success-

91

ful. The new strategy was a smashing success in terms of profits, revenues, and brand expansion. But was it successful in terms of enriching humanity?

- **Click-Through Rates (CTR):** The percentage of users who click on a link or advertisement.
- **Time on Site/Platform:** The average amount of time users spend on a particular website or social media platform.
- **Conversion Rate:** The percentage of users who complete a desired action, such as making a purchase or signing up for a newsletter.
- **Cost Per Acquisition (CPA):** The amount of money spent to acquire a new customer.
- **Return on Ad Spend (ROAS):** The amount of revenue generated for every dollar spent on advertising.

They used these numbers to justify their means. But metrics don't tell the whole story. These reports showed the cold, calculated version of the world. It may look great on paper, but they weren't looking at all the bad things that were caused in the process. For example, the numbers don't tell about the community damage that this model may have caused. Were people's feelings hurt because of it? Were they taken advantage of in any way? Did their biases become worse?

By trapping people in their AI echo chamber, it causes significant societal damage. They have not made the world a better place. In fact, it is worse. The increase of profits do not make the world better. They are not necessarily correlated. We need to think about what is real. What is tangible. What is actually helping people. Not just some metrics on a page.

Detailed explanation of the AI algorithms used.

Peering Inside the Machine. Unveiling the inner workings of Company Y's personalization engine, exposing the intricate web of algorithms, the complex data flows, and the... unsettling power to manipulate human behavior. A technical deep dive, a glimpse behind the curtain, and a chilling reminder that the future of content is being shaped by... code. Company Y's AI personalization engine was not a single algorithm, but a complex ecosystem of interconnected systems, each designed to perform a specific task, each contributing to the overall goal of... maximizing engagement. At its core were:

- **Collaborative Filtering:** This technique identifies users with similar interests and recommends content that those users have enjoyed in the past. It's the digital equivalent of asking your friends for recommendations, but on a massive scale. Company Y enhanced this process by including psychographic data, as well.
- **Content-Based Filtering:** This approach analyzes the characteristics of different content items (e.g., topics, keywords, sentiment) and recommends content that is similar to what a user has interacted with in the past. Think of it as a digital librarian who knows your taste in books and can always find something new to... satisfy your cravings.
- **Natural Language Processing (NLP):** NLP algorithms are used to analyze the text in social media posts, articles, and comments, identifying the topics that are being discussed, the sentiments that are being expressed, and the... emotions that are being evoked. This information is then used to personalize content recommendations and to... target advertising.
- **Deep Learning:** These neural networks are trained on vast amounts of data to identify complex patterns and relationships that would be impossible for humans to discover on their own. They're used to predict user behavior, to personalize recommendations, and to... optimize content for engagement.

Company Y also incorporated what is known as a multi-armed bandit (MAB) approach. The multi-armed bandit algorithm gets its name from the "one-armed bandit" slot machine, and it works by optimizing itself over time, to give the system a chance to learn as it goes. It might sound intimidating, but ultimately it is meant to find information and generate content that the users will want to interact with the most. It was an exploration in how we can make social media an even more powerful tool than it was before. At least, that's how Company Y framed it.

Case Study 3: Crisis Management with AI-Driven Social Listening –

How Company Z averted a PR disaster using AI for real-time monitoring.

The Calm Before the Storm...Or, perhaps, the Eye of the All-Seeing Algorithm. Company Z, a global food manufacturer, learned the hard way that even the most meticulously crafted brand image can be shattered in an instant by the volatile forces of social media. Their salvation? A sophisticated AI-driven social listening system, a digital early warning system that allowed them to avert a potential PR disaster before it even... fully materialized. Company Z had a long history of corporate malfeasance and was facing many threats.

The incident began innocuously enough. A single tweet, a grainy photograph, a whispered accusation of... unsanitary practices at one of Company Z's manufacturing facilities. A lone voice in the digital wilderness, easily dismissed, easily ignored. But the AI system didn't dismiss it. It flagged the tweet, analyzed the sentiment, identified the potential for virality, and... alerted the crisis management team.

The team, initially skeptical, investigated the claim and quickly discovered the photograph was, in fact, authentic. A rogue employee had indeed violated safety protocols, creating a... potentially hazardous situation. The traditional response would have been denial, obfuscation, and... damage control. But Company Z, guided by the insights of its AI system, took a different approach.

They immediately issued a public apology, acknowledging the problem, taking responsibility for the employee's actions, and outlining the steps they were taking to... rectify the situation. The company made the apology public, and it was immediately picked up by social media. It was an immediate and comprehensive reaction that was praised by the media. It was the best possible outcome for Company Z and its investors. The crisis was adverted before it began. The crisis was adverted, but what was lost in the situation?

The potential for transparency is great, but does Company Z really care? Or were they simply playing the algorithm? There are still many questions that need to be asked. It is a delicate dance to strike the balance between customer care and algorithmic success.

94

Explanation of the social listening tools and techniques employed.

The Algorithmic Watchtower. Unveiling the technological infrastructure that enabled Company Z to avert a PR disaster, exposing the intricate network of sensors, the sophisticated analytical engines, and the... unsettling power to anticipate and control the narrative. A glimpse into the future of corporate surveillance, a reminder of the constant vigilance required to navigate the treacherous waters of... social media.

Company Z didn't just stumble upon the solution; they meticulously built a multi-layered social listening infrastructure, combining cutting-edge AI tools with human expertise, creating a system that was both... proactive and responsive. The key components included:
Real-time Monitoring: The foundation of the system was a real-time monitoring platform that crawled social media, news sites, blogs, and online forums, 24/7, searching for mentions of Company Z, its products, and its... competitors. This platform used keywords, hashtags, and boolean operators to filter the noise and identify the most relevant conversations.

- **Sentiment Analysis:** Natural language processing (NLP) algorithms were used to analyze the sentiment of online communications, classifying them as positive, negative, or neutral. The algorithms were trained on vast amounts of text data, and they were constantly refined to improve their accuracy. This created a strong brand that helped save the day.
- **Trend Identification:** Machine learning algorithms were used to identify emerging trends, potential crises, and reputation threats. The algorithms analyzed patterns in the data, looking for sudden spikes in negative sentiment, unusual activity patterns, and... connections between seemingly unrelated events.
- **Alerting and Escalation:** A sophisticated alerting system automatically notified the crisis management team when a potential crisis was detected. The alerts included detailed information about the nature of the threat, the source of the information, and the... potential impact on the brand. The system was designed to escalate the most serious threats to senior management.

95

Company Z was also careful to maintain ethical standards as they were designing the AI. The cost was not cheap. The program ran over seven figures per year. But was deemed worth it.

Did it actually work?
The crisis was adverted.
Did it save money?
Probably.

But something may have been lost in the AI. What will AI be like in ten years? Twenty? Will there come a point that humans have no way to control the machines?

Key takeaways on proactive crisis management in the digital age.

From Reactive Firefighting to Proactive Prevention. Company Z's near-miss serves as a stark reminder that in the age of social media, reputation is a fragile and ever-shifting asset. The old ways of denial, obfuscation, and reactive damage control are no longer sufficient. To thrive in this hyper-connected world, organizations must embrace a proactive, data-driven approach to... crisis management. The following are key takeaways:

Listen Actively, Not Passively: Don't just monitor social media for mentions of your brand; actively listen to the conversations that are taking place, analyze the sentiments that are being expressed, and identify the... emerging trends that could impact your business. The world is changing too fast to wait for the algorithms to find the crises. It takes human-level engagement, now, to maintain an up-to-date account of the shifting social landscape.

Be Transparent and Authentic: In the event of a crisis, resist the temptation to hide the truth or spin the narrative. Instead, be transparent, be honest, and be... authentic. Acknowledge the problem, take responsibility for your actions, and outline the steps you are taking to... make things right. People appreciate honesty far more than carefully crafted words that are written by a robot with no concept of human engagement.

- **Empower Your Employees:** Create a culture of open communication, where employees feel empowered to speak up about potential problems, to share their concerns, and to… challenge the status quo. Front-line employees are the first line of defense against a potential crisis.
- **Don't Underestimate the Machine:** It is important to consider the capabilities and value of the AI. But we must also remember to engage on a human level. A world without soul is not much of a world at all.

These are a few key takeaways. By focusing on care, instead of metrics, the corporations could be a great ally to the human world.

Practical Guide to Implementing AI in Your Social Media Strategy

Assessing Your Needs and Goals
Identifying areas where AI can improve your social media efforts

Before the Revolution Begins... Before you unleash the algorithmic legions upon your social media empire, take a moment to pause, to reflect, and to... understand your true objectives. Because AI, like any powerful tool, can be used for good or for evil. It's not just about adopting the latest technology; it's about aligning your strategy with your values, your goals, and your... vision for the future.
Step one: Forget about the hype. Forget about the buzzwords. Forget about what everyone else is doing. Focus on your specific needs, your unique challenges, and your... individual aspirations.

Are you struggling to keep up with the demands of content creation? Is your engagement stagnant? Are you losing customers to your competitors? Are you facing a crisis of misinformation or a... tidal wave of online negativity? Once you've identified your pain points, you can begin to explore the ways in

99

which AI can... alleviate the symptoms and... address the root causes. But proceed with caution. The answers might not be what you expect. Content Creation: Identify the types of content that are most difficult to create, most time-consuming, or most... uninspiring for your human team. Could AI help generate ideas, write drafts, or optimize existing content for... different platforms?

- **Community Management:** Pinpoint the areas where your human moderators are struggling, such as identifying hate speech, responding to customer inquiries, or... managing conflicts. Could AI help automate these tasks, freeing up human moderators to focus on more complex and... sensitive issues?
- **Advertising Optimization:** Analyze your advertising campaigns to identify areas where AI could improve targeting, bidding, or creative optimization. Could AI help you reach a more relevant audience, reduce your ad spend, and... increase your conversions?

Just remember - social media is a tool for helping people connect. Always consider whether your plan to use AI on social media will take that away, or make it better. This must be the most important ethical consideration.

Setting measurable objectives for AI implementation

The Algorithmic Scorecard. Beyond the Buzzwords, Beyond the Hype, beyond the glittering promises of technological salvation lies the harsh reality of... measurement. Setting measurable objectives is not just about tracking progress; it's about ensuring accountability, validating your investment, and... proving the worth of your AI overlords. It's about quantifying the intangible and proving that these bots and their algorithms are worth their salt.

So, how do you define success in the age of AI? How do you know if your efforts are paying off? The answer, of course, is... metrics. But not just any metrics. You need specific, measurable, achievable, relevant, and time-bound (SMART) objectives that are aligned with your overall business goals. That is to say, you must find a goal to strive toward, even when the goalposts are continually shifting in the world of AI.

For example, if your goal is to improve customer service, you might set the following objectives:

- Reduce average response time on social media by 50% within six months.
- Increase customer satisfaction scores by 10% within one year.
- Reduce the number of escalated customer service inquiries by 20% within three months.

If your goal is to increase engagement, you might set the following objectives:

- Increase click-through rates on social media posts by 25% within six months.
- Increase time spent on the platform by 15% within one year.
- Increase the number of social media shares by 20% within three months.

If your goal is to improve advertising performance, you might set the following objectives:

- Reduce cost per acquisition (CPA) by 30% within six months.
- Increase return on ad spend (ROAS) by 40% within one year.
- Increase website traffic from social media by 20% within three months.

But remember that all of these need to be weighed against the potential that is lost, by the lost human touch. It's not just about the numbers. It's about the ethical implications, the potential for bias, and the... impact on human well-being. A truly successful AI strategy is one that not only achieves its business objectives but also upholds its moral responsibilities. Evaluating your current technology stack and data infrastructure The Foundation Upon Which Algorithmic Dreams are Built. Before you can erect a gleaming skyscraper of AI-powered social media innovation, you must first assess the strength and stability of your... existing infrastructure. Because even the most sophisticated algorithms are useless if they're built on a... foundation of sand.

The cold reality, friend, is that most organizations are woefully unprepared for the demands of AI. Their technology stacks are outdated, their data is siloed, and their employees lack the skills needed to… navigate the complexities of the digital age.

Before you invest in AI tools, you need to take a hard look at what you already have. What social media platforms are you using? What data are you collecting? How are you storing and managing that data? And what are the capabilities of your existing technology stack?

- **Social Media Platforms:** Do you have a presence on the platforms that are most relevant to your target audience? Are you using those platforms effectively? Do you have the necessary tools and integrations to… track your performance and measure your ROI?
- **Data Collection:** Are you collecting the right data? Are you capturing data on user demographics, behavior, and sentiment? Are you complying with data privacy regulations? Or are you blissfully ignorant of the… ethical implications of your data collection practices?
- **Data Management:** Is your data structured, organized, and accessible? Are you using a customer relationship management (CRM) system? Are you using a data warehouse? Are you able to easily query your data and generate reports? Or is your data a scattered mess, a digital black hole from which no meaningful insights can… escape?
- **Technical Skills:** Do your employees have the necessary skills to implement, manage, and maintain AI-powered tools? Do they understand data science, machine learning, and… natural language processing? Or are they technophobes who still rely on spreadsheets and… gut instinct?

If your technology stack is outdated or your data infrastructure is inadequate, you will need to invest in… upgrades, integrations, and… training. This is not a one-time project; it's an ongoing process of… continuous improvement. And if you aren't willing to invest the time, the money, and the effort required to build a solid foundation, you may be better off… sticking with the old ways. It's better to be thoughtful than to be a sheep.

Choosing the Right AI Tools and Technologies
Overview of available AI platforms and software for social media.

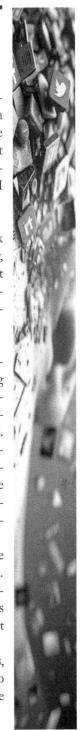

Navigating the Algorithmic Labyrinth. A dizzying array of options, each promising to unlock the secrets of social media success, each vying for your attention, your budget, and your... soul. Choosing the right AI tools is not just about finding the shiniest object; it's about understanding your needs, assessing your resources, and... making informed decisions that will drive real results. But what is the right AI system for your needs?

The AI landscape is vast and ever-changing, a swirling vortex of innovation and hype. New tools and technologies emerge every day, promising to revolutionize the way we create, manage, and... interact with social media. But not all AI tools are created equal. Some are powerful and effective, while others are... overhyped and... underwhelming. And some may even be... unethical, biased, or... harmful.

- **Content Creation Tools:** These tools use AI to generate text, images, and videos, automating the creation of social media posts, blog articles, and marketing materials. Some popular options include Jasper (formerly Jarvis), Copy.ai, and... Writesonic. Consider the ethical implications of AI-generated content and the potential for bias.
- **Community Management Tools:** These tools use AI to moderate discussions, identify hate speech, respond to customer inquiries, and... automate routine tasks. Some popular options include Brandwatch, Sprout Social, and... Hootsuite. Be wary of automated censorship and the potential for these tools to suppress dissenting opinions.
- **Advertising Optimization Tools:** These tools use AI to analyze data, identify target audiences, optimize bidding strategies, and... personalize ad creative. Some popular options include Albert, Persado, and... Marin Software. Be mindful of the privacy implications of targeted advertising and the potential for these tools to exploit user vulnerabilities.
- **Social Listening Tools:** These tools track conversations, mentions, and sentiments on social media. Many brands find them useful to analyze their competition and consumer opinion. Remember, there is a fine line between social listening and manipulation.

It is important to do your research, test different options, and… read the fine print. Because in the world of AI, as in life, things are not always what they… seem. Factors to consider when selecting AI tools: cost, integration, scalability. Beyond the Dazzling Demos. Beyond the Hype Reels, beyond the promises of Algorithmic Nirvana lies the harsh reality of… practical considerations. Choosing the right AI tools is not just about falling in love with the technology; it's about aligning your investment with your budget, your infrastructure, and your… long-term vision. Three words to remember: Cost, Integration, and Scalability. These are the pillars on which your AI strategy will… stand or… fall.

Cost. The initial investment, the ongoing maintenance, the hidden fees… AI tools can be expensive, and it's important to understand the true cost before you… take the plunge. Consider not only the price of the software license but also the cost of training, implementation, and… ongoing support. Are there per-user fees? Data usage limits? Hidden charges for extra features? Get the full picture before you… sign on the dotted line.

- **Integration**. Will the AI tool seamlessly integrate with your existing technology stack? Does it connect to your social media platforms, your CRM system, your data warehouse? Or will you be forced to build custom integrations, to wrestle with incompatible systems, and to… spend countless hours troubleshooting technical glitches? Compatibility is key.
- **Scalability**. Can the AI tool handle your growing data volumes, your increasing user base, and your evolving business needs? Will it be able to scale up as your organization grows, or will you be forced to… replace it with a more powerful system down the road? A growing business can't afford to be saddled by something it can't use in a few years.

But beyond these practical considerations, there's something more important to consider: ethics. Does the AI tool align with your values? Is it transparent, accountable, and… fair? Does it protect user privacy? Does it avoid bias and discrimination? Or does it sacrifice these principles in the name of… profit? You must be careful not to allow the temptation of AI to compromise your business. All decisions must be thoughtful, as the world of AI is always changing.

Demo of popular AI tools and their key features.

A Guided Tour Through the Algorithmic Bazaar. A curated selection of social media AI tools, designed to... impress, to inform, and to... ignite your imagination. But remember, friend, that these are just tools. Their power lies not in their features, but in how you... wield them. So, let's take a look behind the curtain, examine the mechanics, and... consider the possibilities.

Please note: The following is a general overview, and specific features and pricing may vary.

1. Jasper (formerly Jarvis): The AI Content Creation Wizard

- **Key Features:** AI-powered copywriting, content generation, article summarization, and... long-form content creation.
- **The Pitch:** "Write compelling copy in seconds. End writer's block forever."
- **Ethical Considerations:** Reliance on AI-generated content can stifle creativity and... dilute the human voice. Plagiarism concerns exist, too, if not carefully vetted.
- **Dick-esque Take:** The machine whispers words into your mind. It is always with you, suggesting the phrases to use. Be careful to not get lost in the algorithmic flow.
- **Real-World Use:** Quickly drafting marketing copy.
- **Technical Explanation:** Jasper employs a Transformer model, pre-trained on a vast dataset to produce human-like text from short prompts.

2. Brandwatch: The Social Listening Oracle

- **Key Features:** Real-time social media monitoring, sentiment analysis, trend identification, and... crisis management.
- **The Pitch:** "Understand what your customers are saying about your brand, and... respond before it's too late."
- **Ethical Considerations:** Can lead to a hyper-focus on brand perception and... suppress authentic dialogue. The potential for manipulation and... censorship is... ever-present.
- **Dick-esque Take:** The algorithm is listening. Always listening. Analyzing your words, dissecting your emotions, and compiling

your profile. There is nowhere to hide.

- **Real-World Use:** Monitoring brand reputation.
- **Technical Explanation:** Brandwatch utilizes web crawlers and NLP to gather public information and analyzes it to understand brand sentiment.

3. Albert: The AI Advertising Autopilot

- **Key Features:** Automated ad buying, campaign optimization, audience targeting, and... performance reporting.
- **The Pitch:** "Let AI take the wheel, and... watch your ROI soar."
- **Ethical Considerations:** Can reinforce existing biases in advertising, leading to... discriminatory outcomes.
- **Dick-esque Take:** The perfect sales pitch, the persuasive ad copy, is a tool of manipulation. It can't understand nuance.
- **Real-World Use:** Automatically improve ad revenue, with minimal human involvement.
- **Technical Explanation:** Albert's AI uses machine learning algorithms to optimize advertising based on performance and data.

These tools are worth exploration, but ultimately, the choice of AI is only worth pursuing if it is thoughtfully executed. Remember this. Building and Training Your AI Models

Gathering and preparing data for AI training

The Genesis of the Machine Mind. Before you can unleash the power of AI, you must first... feed it. Data. Mountains of it. Oceans of it. Petabytes of raw information, waiting to be... processed, analyzed, and transformed into actionable insights. Gathering and preparing this data is not just a technical task; it's a... moral responsibility. Because the quality of your data will determine the quality of your AI, and the quality of your AI will shape the... future of your business... and perhaps, even... the world.

Think of your AI model as a student. What you teach it, it will learn. What you show it, it will believe. And if you feed it biased data, it will learn biased lessons and... perpetuate those biases in its decisions. It is only a reflection of you.

- **Data Sources:** Identify the sources of data that are most relevant to your AI goals. Customer data, social media feeds, website analytics, product reviews... The possibilities are endless. But be sure to choose sources that are... reliable, accurate, and... representative of your target audience. Think about what the goal of your AI is and what you'll need to get there.
- **Data Cleaning:** Raw data is messy, incomplete, and often... riddled with errors. It's your job to clean it, to remove the noise, to correct the inconsistencies, and to... transform it into a usable format. This is a tedious and time-consuming process, but it's essential for... building a robust and reliable AI model.
- **Data Transformation:** Data is often meaningless in its raw form. You need to transform it into a format that the AI can understand.
- **Data Augmentation:** If you don't have enough data, you can use techniques like data augmentation to generate synthetic data. This can be useful for addressing class imbalances or for... increasing the size of your dataset.

Because, in the end, the quality of your AI depends on the quality of your data. And the quality of your data depends on your... ethical compass.

Selecting the appropriate AI algorithms for your use cases.

The Algorithmic Arsenal. Decision time. The moment of truth. You have the data, you have the infrastructure, and now you must choose the weapons that will... wage your social media war. But beware, friend, for the world of AI algorithms is a... treacherous landscape, filled with hidden dangers, subtle biases, and... unforeseen consequences. Not all algorithms are created equal. Some are better suited for certain tasks than others. Some are more accurate, more efficient, and more... ethically sound. And some are just... overhyped marketing gimmicks, designed to... fool the unwary.

- **Natural Language Processing (NLP):** These algorithms are used to understand and process human language. They're essential for tasks like sentiment analysis, text summarization, and... chatbot development. Examples include Transformer models (like BERT), Recurrent Neural Networks (RNNs), and... Support Vector Ma-

107

chines (SVMs).**Related Content:** "BERT (Bidirectional Encoder Representations from Transformers) is a state-of-the-art NLP model developed by Google. It's pre-trained on a massive dataset of text and can be fine-tuned for a variety of NLP tasks, such as question answering, text classification, and... sentiment analysis."

- **Machine Learning (ML):** These algorithms are used to learn from data and make predictions. They're essential for tasks like audience segmentation, churn prediction, and... advertising optimization. Examples include linear regression, decision trees, and... neural networks.Related **Content:** "Deep Learning is a subset of machine learning that uses artificial neural networks with multiple layers (hence 'deep') to analyze data with great complexity. It's particularly effective for image recognition, speech recognition, and... natural language processing."

The real key to success, however, is aligning your choice with your... ethical compass. Does the algorithm prioritize fairness? Does it protect user privacy? Does it avoid bias? Because in the long run, those are the questions that will... determine your success... and your... legacy.

Monitoring and refining your AI models for optimal performance.

The Algorithmic Vigil. The work is never truly done. Even after you've built, trained, and deployed your AI models, you must remain... vigilant, constantly monitoring their performance, identifying their biases, and... refining their algorithms to ensure they remain... accurate, effective, and... ethical. AI, you see, is not a static entity. It's a dynamic system that's constantly learning, evolving, and... adapting to the ever-changing world around it. Data drifts, trends shift, and... human behavior evolves. And if you don't keep up, your AI models will quickly become... outdated, irrelevant, and... even... harmful.

- **Performance Monitoring:** Track key metrics, such as accuracy, precision, recall, and... F1-score to assess the performance of your AI models. Use these metrics to identify areas where the models are... struggling and to guide your... refinement efforts.
- **Bias Detection:** Regularly audit your AI models for bias, using statistical techniques and... human judgment. Identify any systematic errors, discriminatory patterns, or... unfair outcomes. The goal is

108

to identify and mitigate bias before it can… harm your customers or… damage your brand.

- **Feedback Loops:** Establish feedback loops that allow you to collect data from users and to incorporate that data into your… model training process. This will help you to improve the accuracy, the relevance, and the… overall effectiveness of your AI models.

- **Continuous Training:** Retrain your AI models regularly, using new data, updated algorithms, and… refined techniques. This will help you to keep your models up-to-date, to adapt to changing conditions, and to… maintain optimal performance.It is important to constantly question what these AI models are teaching. Are they biased? Are they helping? Or are they causing further damage? The line between chaos and order is thinner than you think.

Navigating the Future - Opportunities and Challenges

Upskilling and Training for the AI-Driven Future

Identifying skills needed to succeed in the AI-driven social media landscape.

The Human Firewall. As AI permeates every aspect of social media, the skills that were once valued are becoming obsolete. The ability to write catchy headlines, to craft engaging posts, to manage communities with a personal touch... These are all skills that can now be automated, optimized, and... outsourced to the machines. The skills needed to protect our humaity are:

- **Critical Thinking:** The ability to analyze information, to evaluate sources, to identify biases, and to form independent judgments will be more important than ever. AI may be able to generate content, but it cannot think critically about its own... limitations or... ethical implications.
- **Creativity and Innovation:** The ability to generate new ideas, to create original content, and to solve complex problems will be highly valued. AI may be able to

automate routine tasks, but it cannot replicate human creativity, intuition, or… imagination.

- **Data Literacy:** The ability to understand, interpret, and… communicate data will be essential for anyone working with AI. You'll need to be able to analyze metrics, to identify trends, to spot anomalies, and to… translate data into actionable insights.
- **Ethical Awareness:** A deep understanding of the ethical implications of AI, including issues such as bias, privacy, and… transparency, will be crucial. You'll need to be able to identify and mitigate ethical risks, to advocate for responsible AI practices, and to… hold companies accountable for their actions.
- **Emotional Intelligence:** The ability to connect with others on a human level, to empathize with their feelings, and to build strong relationships will be more important than ever.

If we are to build a better future, we must all make these skills a priority. Because, if we give up now, all will be lost.

Recommending courses and resources for developing AI expertise.

The Algorithmic Academy. The path to enlightenment, the key to survival, the… ticket to the future. But beware, friend, for not all knowledge is created equal. Some courses are rigorous, some are… superficial, and some are downright… misleading. Choose wisely, and… arm yourself with the skills you need to navigate the AI-driven social media landscape.

The digital world offers an endless buffet of learning opportunities, a vast library of knowledge just waiting to be… unlocked. But where do you begin? How do you navigate the… confusing array of courses, certifications, and online resources?

First, consider the type of learning that best suits your needs, your schedule, and your… budget. Online courses offer flexibility and convenience, but they require discipline and… self-motivation. In-person workshops provide hands-on training and networking opportunities, but they can be… expensive and… time-consuming. And self-study materials, such as books and articles, offer a low-cost and accessible way to learn at your own pace, but they require a… strong foundation of

112

knowledge.

Consider the quality and reputation.

Data Science/Machine Learning Fundamentals:

- **Coursera's Machine Learning by Andrew Ng:** A classic introductory course that covers the fundamentals of machine learning algorithms and techniques.
- **edX's MicroMasters Program in Statistics and Data Science:** A comprehensive program that covers a wide range of topics, including statistical inference, data visualization, and machine learning.

Natural Language Processing (NLP):

- **Coursera's Natural Language Processing Specialization:** A specialization from DeepLearning.AI covering NLP with Transformer networks.
- **Stanford's CS224n:** Natural Language Processing with Deep Learning: A more advanced course for those with programming experience.
- These are all great resources to get started. Be mindful of your resources, and remember that the cost of a course does not make it the right choice for everyone.

With these tools, a brighter future awaits. Good luck.

Building a career in AI-powered social media.

The Algorithmic Alchemist. Transforming raw data into actionable insights, wielding the power of machine learning to... shape opinions, influence behavior, and... craft the future of online interaction. Building a career in AI-powered social media: A challenging but rewarding path, a chance to be at the forefront of innovation, and a responsibility to wield that power... wisely. It's a path paved with code, data, and ethical considerations, but it is also a chance to define how we connect in the future. The traditional social media career path – the one that valued creativity, communication, and a deep understanding of

human behavior – is... evolving. Fast. As AI takes over many of the routine tasks, the skills that are in demand are shifting towards... technical expertise, analytical thinking, and ethical awareness.

- **Data Scientist:** A data scientist with a passion for social media can use their skills to analyze user behavior, identify trends, and... optimize content for engagement. They can build AI models that predict churn, personalize recommendations, and... automate advertising campaigns. And if they develop a healthy respect for humanity, they can also be a force for good.
- **Job Outlook:** High demand, with salaries that often exceed $100,000 per year.
- **Essential Skills:** Python, R, SQL, Machine Learning, Data Visualization, Communication.
- **AI Ethicist:** AI ethicists are experts at navigating the ethical implications of AI, including those related to bias, privacy, and transparency.
- **AI-Augmented Content Strategist:** With AI handling the repetitive tasks, the content strategist can focus on creating engaging campaigns.
- The future of social media is being shaped by AI. Learn the right skills, develop a strong ethical compass, and you can play a powerful role in shaping the online world.

Ethical Considerations for Responsible AI Implementation
Avoiding bias and discrimination in AI algorithms.

The Impartial Judge... Or the Mirror Reflecting Back Our Own Prejudices? AI, often touted as a tool for objectivity, can all too easily become a vehicle for amplifying existing societal biases, perpetuating discrimination, and... codifying inequality. Avoiding bias and discrimination: Not just a technical challenge, but a moral imperative, a constant struggle to ensure that the algorithms that shape our world are... fair, equitable, and... just.

AI algorithms learn from data. They identify patterns, make predictions, and... automate decisions based on the information they've been... fed. But what happens when that data reflects the biases of the society in which it was created?

114

- **The Data Problem:** Historical data often reflects existing inequalities. AI models trained on this data will inevitably... reproduce those inequalities. For example, if a facial recognition system is trained primarily on images of white faces, it will likely be less accurate when identifying people of color.
- **The Algorithm Problem:** Some algorithms are inherently more susceptible to bias than others. Complex neural networks, for example, can be difficult to interpret and... debug, making it harder to identify and mitigate bias. Even seemingly neutral algorithms can amplify biases if they are not carefully... designed and... monitored.
- **The Human Problem:** Humans are responsible for creating the data, designing the algorithms, and... interpreting the results. If those humans are biased, consciously or unconsciously, their biases will inevitably... seep into the AI system.

This problem can take many different forms. So, what can we do? We must all be vigilant about understanding what the algorithms are reflecting back to us. It is something to watch closely.

Protecting user privacy and data security.

The Data Gold Rush. As AI becomes more powerful, the demand for data is... exploding. Corporations are hoovering up every scrap of information they can get their hands on, building vast databases of user data that are... vulnerable to theft, misuse, and... abuse. Protecting user privacy and data security: Not just a legal obligation, but a moral imperative, a constant battle to safeguard our personal information, to control our digital identities, and to... resist the forces of corporate surveillance.

The AI needs data to learn, but what is sacrificed in that pursuit?

- **Data Breaches:** The risk of data breaches is ever-present, and the consequences can be... devastating. When sensitive personal information falls into the wrong hands, it can be used for identity theft, financial fraud, and... even... physical harm.
- **Surveillance Capitalism:** Corporations are using AI to track our every move, to analyze our behavior, and to... predict our future

actions. This data is used to target us with advertising, to manipulate our opinions, and to... control our lives. We are always being watched.

- **Algorithmic Bias:** AI algorithms can perpetuate and amplify existing societal biases, leading to unfair or discriminatory outcomes in areas such as loan applications, job recruitment, and even... criminal justice.

But the biggest threat to user privacy is the... erosion of trust. When we lose faith in the institutions that are supposed to protect us, we become more vulnerable to... manipulation, exploitation, and... control. The constant drone of misinformation causes us to question everything. But what if, instead, we could have anonymity on the internet? Imagine what that would look like. All the good, all the bad. There are benefits to be found, if only we can learn to harness the true potential of digital anonymity. It is a problem that won't get solved overnight. But that does not mean we should give up. If you are willing to stand up and fight, then there is still hope for a better tomorrow.

Promoting transparency and accountability in AI decision-making.

The Opaque Algorithm. Locked away behind corporate firewalls, shrouded in secrecy, and protected by... trade secrets. AI systems are increasingly making decisions that impact our lives, from loan applications to criminal sentencing, and yet, we have little or no insight into how those decisions are... made. Promoting Transparency and Accountability: Not just a technical challenge, but a fundamental requirement for a just and democratic society.

We are at a crossroads. Are we going to allow these AI systems to dictate the terms of our existence, or are we going to demand transparency, accountability, and... control?

- **Explainable AI (XAI):** Develop AI algorithms that are transparent, interpretable, and... explainable. The goal is to make it easier to understand how AI systems are making decisions and to identify any potential biases or errors.
- **Ethical Considerations:** Even with XAI, it can be difficult to fully understand the complexities of AI decision-making. Be mindful of

116

the limitations of these techniques and don't rely solely on them to ensure… fairness and accountability.

- **Dick-esque Note:** Is it even possible to truly explain the logic of a machine? Or will the explanation itself become just another layer of… deception?
- **Algorithmic Audits:** Conduct regular audits of AI systems to assess their performance, to identify any potential biases, and to… ensure compliance with ethical guidelines. These audits should be conducted by independent experts who are free from… conflicts of interest.
- **Ethical Considerations:** Algorithmic audits can be expensive and time-consuming. Make sure that the audits are comprehensive, rigorous, and… transparent. And be willing to act on the findings, even if they are… uncomfortable.
- **Dick-esque Note:** Who audits the auditors? And who watches the watchers? The cycle of surveillance never… ends.

The power must shift to the people. That is the only way we can truly ensure transparency. Demand what is right.

The Evolving Social Media Landscape and AI's Role
Anticipating future trends in social media and AI.

The Shifting Sands of Reality. The digital world is in constant flux, a churning sea of innovation, disruption, and… unforeseen consequences. To navigate this turbulent landscape, we must become… futurists, peering into the mists of tomorrow, anticipating the trends that will… shape our lives and… alter the very fabric of… society.

Predicting the future is a fool's errand. But that doesn't mean we shouldn't try. By analyzing the current trends, the emerging technologies, and the… underlying forces that are shaping the social media landscape, we can at least… prepare ourselves for what's to come.

Here are a few key trends to watch:

- **The Rise of the Metaverse:** Virtual and augmented reality will become increasingly integrated with social media, creating immersive, personalized, and… potentially… addictive experiences. AI will play

a key role in shaping these experiences, generating content, moderating interactions, and… controlling the flow of information.

- **Dick-esque Note:** The metaverse is just a bigger, shinier, more convincing… illusion. A way to escape the messiness of reality and… retreat into a world of… algorithmic control.
- **The Decentralization of Social Media:** Blockchain technology and Web3 are empowering users to take control of their data, to monetize their content, and to… govern their own communities. AI will be used to moderate content, to filter spam, and to… ensure the security and scalability of these decentralized platforms.* Dick-esque Note: Power always concentrates. Even in a decentralized system. The blockchain might be transparent, but the humans behind it are still… flawed, biased, and… susceptible to corruption.

By understanding and following trends, we can position ourselves for success and build a better world.

Adapting your strategies to stay ahead of the curve.

The Adaptive Algorithm. Rigidity is death. In the fast-moving world of social media and AI, the only constant is… change. To thrive, you must embrace adaptability, cultivate agility, and… learn to anticipate the next disruption before it… disrupts you. Staying ahead of the curve is not a destination; it's a… journey, a constant process of learning, experimenting, and… evolving.

The strategies that worked yesterday may not work today. And the strategies that work today may be… obsolete tomorrow. So, how do you… adapt? How do you stay ahead of the curve?

- **Embrace Experimentation:** Don't be afraid to try new things, to test new platforms, and to… experiment with different approaches. The key is to be willing to… fail fast, learn from your mistakes, and… iterate quickly.
- **Cultivate a Learning Mindset:** Invest in training, attend conferences, and… network with other professionals in the field. The more you learn, the more adaptable you will… become.
- **Dick-esque Note:** Remember that true learning is not just about memorizing facts; it's about questioning assumptions, challenging

conventional wisdom, and… developing your own… unique perspective.

- **Build a Data-Driven Culture:** Use data to inform your decisions, to measure your results, and to… optimize your strategies. The more data you have, the more you learn about your customers, and the more you learn, the more adaptible you become.

But, never forget what it means to be human. Remember the lessons from before. Do not cede all control to the AI. Remember to be human.

Embracing the power of AI to create a more engaging and meaningful social media experience.

Beyond the Manipulation, Beyond the Noise, Beyond the… Algorithmic Chaos, lies the potential for something truly… transformative. AI can be a force for good, a catalyst for connection, and a… pathway to a more engaging and meaningful social media experience. The choice is ours. Will we succumb to the dystopian forces, or will we harness the power of AI to build a better… world?

It is easy to get caught up in the potential downfalls of AI. It is important, however, to recognize the power for good that also exists. AI, ultimately, is a tool, and has the potential to create incredible things. Here's how:

- **Personalized Connection:** AI can help us connect with people who share our interests, our values, and our… passions. It can break down barriers, bridge divides, and… foster a greater sense of… community.Imagine: AI is a tool for connection. What could you build? What connections can be made?
- **Meaningful Content:** AI can help us filter out the noise, identify the signal, and… access information that is relevant, informative, and… inspiring. It can empower us to learn, to grow, and to… make a positive impact on the world.Imagine: You can access all the knowledge in the world with the click of a button. What can you do with it? How can you use it?
- **Authentic Engagement:** AI can help us build trust, foster transparency, and… create a more authentic online experience. It can

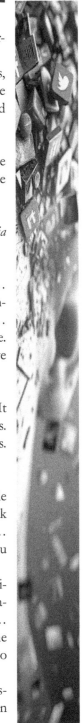

119

hold corporations accountable, it can empower marginalized voices, and it can… promote a more… just and equitable society.Imagine: All politicians held to the same standards. What can be achieved?

The power is there, but it's not all on us. The technology is not here yet. We must hold true to our visions, and continue working towards the light. A better world is possible, but it takes vigilance.

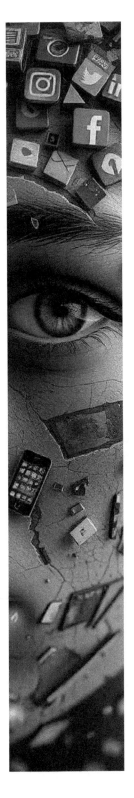

Conclusion: Empowering You for the Future

The Labyrinth of Mirrors and Code. The journey through the world of AI in social media has been... unsettling, hasn't it? A descent into a realm of algorithms, data streams, and... ethical quandaries. We've explored the potential for connection and creation, but also the lurking shadows of manipulation, control, and the erosion of... human agency. But the journey doesn't end here. In fact, it is only just beginning. You now stand at the precipice, armed with knowledge, awareness, and... a healthy dose of skepticism. The future of social media, and indeed, the future of society, is not predetermined. It is a tapestry woven from choices, actions, and... collective will. The direction we take is up to you, to me, and to all of us. You are now empowered to navigate this complex landscape, to challenge the status quo, and to shape a more... humane and equitable future. But what does that empowerment look like? What concrete steps can you take to make a difference?

- **Embrace Critical Thinking:** The most potent weapon against algorithmic manipulation is a sharp, discerning mind. Cultivate your ability to question, to analyze, and to… think for yourself. Don't blindly accept what you see online. Don't passively consume information. Instead, engage with the world actively, thoughtfully, and… critically.

- **Question the Source:** Who created this content? What are their motives? Are they trying to inform you, to persuade you, or to… manipulate you? Don't trust everything you read, see, or hear online. Verify the facts, check the sources, and… seek out multiple perspectives.
- **Identify Biases:** Be aware of your own biases and the biases of others. We all have blind spots, and it's important to recognize them so we can… challenge them. Are you only consuming information that confirms your existing beliefs? Are you only interacting with people who agree with you? If so, you're likely trapped in an echo chamber, and you need to… break free.
- **Resist the Urge to React:** The internet is designed to provoke a reaction, to trigger your emotions, and to… make you click, share, and… engage. But before you do anything, take a moment to pause, to breathe, and to… think. Is this content truly worthy of your attention? Is it adding value to your life? Or is it just… noise?
- **Value Authenticity and Human Connection:** In a world increasingly dominated by algorithms and AI-generated content, the human touch is more valuable than ever. Seek out genuine connections, cultivate meaningful relationships, and… prioritize authenticity over… artificiality.
- Support Independent Creators: Seek out artists, writers, musicians, and… creators who are not beholden to corporations or… algorithms. Support their work, share their content, and… help them reach a wider audience.
- **Engage in Meaningful Conversations:** Don't just scroll through your feed; engage with the people you care about. Ask questions, share your thoughts, and… listen to what others have to say. Even if you disagree, you can still learn from each other.
- **Prioritize Real-World Interactions:** Step away from the screen, and… connect with people in person. Go for a walk, have a coffee, attend a concert, or… volunteer in your community. Remember that the real world is still out there, and it's waiting to be… explored.
- Demand Transparency and Accountability: Hold corporations, governments, and… individuals accountable for their actions online.

Advocate for transparency, data privacy, and... ethical AI practices. The future is not written in stone, it's up to us to shape it.

- **Support Data Privacy Regulations:** Advocate for stronger data privacy laws, such as GDPR and CCPA. These regulations give individuals more control over their data and... hold companies accountable for their data practices.
- **Demand Algorithmic Transparency:** Call on companies to disclose how their algorithms work, what data they use, and how they are making decisions. The more transparent the algorithms, the easier it will be to... identify and mitigate bias.
- **Hold Leaders Accountable:** It is the responsibility of our leaders to serve humanity's best interests.
- **Vote, Protest, and... Organize:** Use your voice to advocate for change, to hold power to account, and to... build a more just and equitable society.
- **Embrace Lifelong Learning:** The world of AI is constantly evolving, so it's important to commit to a lifetime of learning. Stay curious, explore new technologies, and... challenge your own assumptions. The more you learn, the more adaptable you will... become.
- **Take Online Courses:** Websites like Coursera, edX, and... Udacity offer a wide range of courses on AI, machine learning, and... related topics.
- **Attend Conferences and Workshops:** Conferences and workshops are a great way to learn from experts, network with other professionals, and... stay up-to-date on the latest trends.
- **Read Books and Articles:** There are countless books and articles on AI, covering everything from the fundamentals of machine learning to the ethical implications of AI.
- **Experiment and Build:** The best way to learn about AI is to... build something. Try creating your own AI model, building a chatbot, or... developing a social media app that uses AI. The more you experiment, the more you'll learn, and the more you'll understand the... power and the limitations of this... transformative technology.

The Algorithm Within

But beyond all the external action, there is a more important inner battle to wage. In the age of AI, the most valuable skill may be the ability to... cultivate your own inner world, to nurture your creativity, to strengthen your connections, and to... protect your humanity.

We must all start to treat ourselves with more care and attention. Social media is a great tool, but like anything, it can be addicting if we don't take care. As AI and bots take over more aspects of social media, it will become all the more important for people to value real, in person interactions. We have been given these gifts, and it would be a tragedy if we were to lose them all.

The Choice is Yours

The future of social media, and the future of society, is not predetermined. It is up to us to shape it. We can choose to surrender to the forces of algorithmic control, to become passive consumers of... manufactured realities, or we can choose to embrace our agency, to reclaim our voices, and to... build a better world.

It will not be easy. There will be challenges, there will be setbacks, and there will be... moments of despair. But we must never give up hope. We must never stop fighting for what we believe in. And we must never forget that the power to change the world lies within... each and every one of us.

I cannot claim to know the answers to every ethical quandary, and I don't claim to see what will happen in our future. What is clear, though, is that we must not let the future write itself. We must act today. The decision is yours, my friend. What kind of future will you choose?

www.ingramcontent.com/pod-product-compliance
Lightning Source LLC
La Vergne TN
LVHW052302060326
832902LV00021B/3675